HAPPINESS
IS YOUR CREATION

Also by Swami Rama

BOOKS:

Living With the Himalayan Masters
The Art of Joyful Living
Love Whispers
Meditation and Its Practice
The Royal Path: Practical Lessons on Yoga
Love and Family Life
A Practical Guide to Holistic Health
Path of Fire and Light, Vol. I and II
Spirituality: Transformation Within & Without
The Valmiki Ramayana Retold in Verse, Vol. I and II
Book of Wisdom: Ishopanishad
Celestial Song/Gobind Geet
Choosing A Path
Freedom from the Bondage of Karma
Perennial Psychology of the Bhagavad Gita
Wisdom of the Ancient Sages: Mundaka Upanishad
Japji: Meditation in Sikhism
Nitnem: Spiritual Practices of Sikhism
Philosophy/Faith of Sikhism
Sikh Gurus—Lives and Teachings
Freedom From Fear
Mantra, Tantra, & Miracles
On the Spiritual Path
Humble Happy & Wise

SWAMI RAMA ALSO CO-AUTHORED:

Joints and Glands Exercises
Meditation and Christianity
Science of Breath
Yoga and Psychotherapy

AUDIO & VIDEO

Guided Meditation for Beginners
A Guide to Intermediate Meditation
A First Step Toward Advanced Meditation
Guided Meditation for Initiates
Inner Peace in a Troubled World
Stressless Living
Spiritual Origins of Health
Finding Meaning in Life
How to Tread the Path of Superconscious Meditation

HAPPINESS
IS YOUR CREATION

Swami Rama

COMPILED BY
PANDIT RAJMANI TIGUNAIT, PH.D.

HIMALAYAN INSTITUTE®
PRESS
HONESDALE, PENNSYLVANIA, USA

Himalayan Institute Press
952 Bethany Turnpike
Honesdale, PA 18431

www.HimalayanInstitute.org

09   08   07   06   05   6 5 4 3 2   1

Printed in China

Cover design by Stefan Gutermuth
Interior design and electronic production by Joan G. Gillner

The paper used in this publication meets the minimum
requirements of American National Standard for Information
Sciences—Permanence of Paper for Printed Library Materials,
ANSI Z39.48-1984.

Library of Congress Cataloging-in-Publication Data

Rama, Swami, 1925-1996
    Happiness is your creation / by Swami Rama ; compiled by
Rajmani Tigunait.
        p. cm.
    ISBN-13: 978-0-89389-246-3
    ISBN-10: 089389-246-7
     0-89389-246-7 (trade pbk. : alk. paper)
    1. Yoga. 2. Meditation. 3. Spiritual life. I. Tigunait, Rajmani,
1953- II. Title.
    B132.Y6R338 2005
    294.5'436—dc22
                                                    2005000646

Contents

Introduction

THIS BOOK, *HAPPINESS IS YOUR CREATION*, IS A living testimony of a man who made happiness his lasting companion. His name is Swami Rama (whom I lovingly call Swamiji), my master, my guide who filled my heart with the conviction that happiness is the only wealth worth acquiring, and all other forms of possession—power, money, prestige—can perform their magic only when happiness breathes life into them.

I lived with this man for twenty years. In this long span of time, I saw how hard he worked and yet how relaxed he was; how complex were the projects that he undertook and yet how tranquil he remained. An aura of joy surrounded him whether he lived in the Himalayan caves or fancy hotels of Tokyo or New York. He was a man who, in the face of death, could at once laugh, make jokes, issue directives to administer a multinational organization, the Himalayan Institute, and instruct students on their inner voyage. As he lay on his deathbed, I saw his face gleaming with a joy not seen before. Puzzled, I asked him, "Swamiji, these days I see you happier than ever before. Why is that?"

With a twinkle in his eyes, he answered, "I used to play in her courtyard. Now She is calling me to play in her lap. That makes me exceedingly happy."

Then he paused for a moment and spoke again. "You are a creation of God, but happiness is your creation. You are equipped with everything that you need to live a happy life. Your only job is to discover the source of happiness within and infuse your surroundings with that inner happiness."

Then, referring to my daughter, who lived in a boarding school just an hour away from him, Swamiji asked, "Where is the little one? When is she coming to visit me?"

My wife and I brought our eight-year-old daughter from the school. As soon as she saw him, she ran to him and climbed into his lap. Swamiji gave her a biscuit. Holding the treat in her hand, she said, "Baba, why are you so thin and weak?"

"Because I am not eating anything these days," he responded.

In her innocence, she inquired, "Why aren't you eating?"

With the same innocence, he answered, "Because I have finished all the food that has been allotted to me, so there is no food left for me."

At this, she spontaneously put that biscuit in his mouth and said, "So . . . you can share some of mine!"

"Since you said so," he said and took a small bite. "I am now full. How old are you?"

When she answered, "Eight," he said, "You know, on your sixteenth birthday, I am going to throw you the biggest birthday party."

"Where, Baba?"

"At my master's home."

"Where does your master live?" she asked.

"At Mount Kailash."

Without knowing the context of the conversation, the little girl giggled. "So, Baba, when are you going to your master's home?"

He said, "Soon after you go to school."

"But Baba, I don't know how to reach your master's home."

Looking at me he said, "I have given your papa the address of my master."

When he dismissed her, the little girl ran out of the room, dancing and declaring to everyone outside, "Baba is going to visit his master, and Baba will give my birthday party at his master's home!"

Then Swamiji looked at my wife and I and said, "How beautiful and pure she is."

This last encounter with him threw me into a deep state of contemplation: How can a person, knowing that he is dying, be so full of cheerfulness and enthusiasm? How can a person about to close his eyes forever see beauty in everything? How, while lying on his deathbed, can he, with so much confidence, promise to throw a birthday party for a little girl eight years from today? What is the state of consciousness of this man, and how did he acquire it? My twenty years of life with him flashed before my eyes, and I heard him lecturing in the auditorium of the Himalayan Institute:

> *"A happy mind is the source of all healing powers. A person with a happy mind is full of enthusiasm, courage, and self-motivation. A person with a happy mind is free from all complaints. Cultivating a joyful mind is the greatest of all spiritual practices. All human beings, regardless of whether they come from the East or the West, are equally in need of happiness. According to the yogis, happiness is always preceded by peace. A quiet mind is the foundation for cultivating a joyful mind. Mental quietude depends on one of the greatest virtues: inner purity. Without inner purity, we suffer from inner poverty."*

Over the next several months, my heart was flooded by his words, and I spent many hours contemplating what they meant. I realized how right he was when, on many occasions, he told his students:

"You are a human being. You must not say that something is beyond your capacity. You can accomplish anything you wish. In you, nature has deposited her best gifts, the gift of intelligence, willpower, determination, and the power of discrimination. Have trust in yourself and in your self-effort. Put your whole heart into your endeavor, and it is guaranteed that divine grace will come to your aid. Remember, God created humans in his own image. This is not a metaphor. This is a statement regarding the perennial truth. You are not just the reflection of God; you are a replica of God. If God means creator, then the creator's creativity is in you. If God means beauty, then that beauty is you, and is in you. If God means love, then that love is you. If God means the power to be and the power to become, then that power is you. Therefore, you have the capacity to become whatever you wish."

This is what Swami Rama, his teachings, and this book are all about.

— Chapter One —

Living with Purpose

A HUMAN BEING IS A CITIZEN OF TWO WORLDS: the world within and the world outside. Some work hard and thrive in the external world, but lacking access to the inner dimensions of life, they suffer from spiritual poverty. Some, on the other hand, place emphasis only on their spiritual growth and go on struggling in the worldly domain. The key to happiness lies in bridging these two worlds. In my long journey, I have met people from all walks of life— businessmen, monks, writers, educators, politicians, and professionals of all kinds. But rarely have I met those who were satisfied with what they had.

Wherever I went, I often found one thing missing— contentment. I pondered why. I read scriptures; I sat at the feet of masters and asked them why people are unhappy. After a long search and ample self-reflection, I concluded that most people do not know that they are residents of two worlds, and that they can only be happy if they have access to both worlds simultaneously. Progress in one area of life is not enough.

We can go on amassing great wealth; we can go on acquiring great power. But a lack of conviction in ourselves makes the ground beneath our feet shaky. We can cultivate conviction in ourselves only when we know who we are, where we come from, what we are supposed to do here, and where we go after we die. In the search to find answers to these inherent questions, we begin to notice that the reality within is far more powerful than the world of projection in which we live. Our lack of knowledge regarding this inner reality is what makes us feel incomplete.

In this world, there are three kinds of people: time-oriented people, ambition-driven people, and purpose-oriented people. Time-oriented people are those who live in the world without understanding why. They have no vision of the future; they live in a world of fantasy. They entertain themselves by glorifying their heroes and reminiscing about the past. Their goals and objectives are set by others; their heaven and hell are defined by others. Such people always remain victims of fear and temptation; in fact, they are run by fear and temptation. Although such people may be physically healthy, they are far from happy.

Then there are the ambition-driven people. To a certain extent, they can physically and mentally discipline themselves. They are thoughtful people; they look at the past and the present and then try to envision their future. But lacking a deeper understanding of the inner dimensions of life, their vision of the future remains limited. They decide the course of their actions and perform their duties in light of the reality that is right before their eyes. Quite often, such people gain success in the external world. They become rich and prosperous. They gain distinction in limited areas of worldly existence. Their success in the external world, however, may not bring true happiness. At some point, they wonder what else there is to be achieved. It is in such people's lives that there comes a turning point. They grasp the gifts that the present offers, and by using those gifts they change the direction of their quest. Once that happens, it is certain that they will achieve the highest goal of life—the self-realization that brings with it the understanding of their relationship with the world, on one hand, and with the Lord of Life on the other.

Another category of people are those who, right from the very beginning of their quest, pay attention to the higher purpose and goal of life. My master used to call such people "the blessed ones." They look at the past, not with the intention of brooding on it, but rather to enrich the present with the lessons of the past. Their every single thought, speech, and action is focused on the highest goal. Their simplest actions and most complex endeavors have only one goal—to live peacefully and happily and to attain complete knowledge of themselves. They do not need to run after happiness, for happiness follows them. Their clear understanding of themselves, their role in the world, and a clear vision of their destination infuse their actions with such a degree of satisfaction that they do not seek any reward from them. Such people are happy here and now. They are the torchbearers of human civilization. Those who recognize and seek guidance from these torchbearers, too, are fortunate.

The great masters of the past understood that a human being is neither body nor mind alone. Rather, a human being is a combination of both. They also knew the force that holds the body and mind together. They called that force *prana*, the vital energy. Beyond body, mind, and vital force lies the pure consciousness. These masters dedicated their lives to understanding which part of us is subject to death, decay, and destruction, and which part of us is immortal; which part of us has a beginning and end, and which part of us has no beginning and no end. Thousands of years of research and experimentation led them to conclude that consciousness is immortal. The rest—body, breath, and mind—belongs to the mortal part of us.

However, to live a healthy and happy life on this plane requires that both the immortal and mortal parts of us remain fully united and that these two aspects support and nurture each other. In the search for immortality, if we ignore our body, breath, and mind, we are bound to suffer. In search of physical comfort and sense pleasure, if we ignore the spiritual part of ourselves, then, too, we are bound to suffer. This realization led the masters to design a holistic path. By following this holistic path, we learn to take care of our body, breath, mind, and consciousness. This is the most complete path for healing and nurturing ourselves at every level. Yogis call it the path of *raja yoga*. Mystics call it *adhyatma yoga*.

The masters of raja yoga proclaim that the body is the greatest gift we have. A healthy body is absolutely necessary for cultivating and retaining a peaceful mind, but the body is merely a covering for the mind. The body is a tool meant to serve the purpose of the mind and soul. The whole of the body is in the mind, but the whole of the mind is not in the body. Only part of the mind is dependent on physical comforts and pleasures for its happiness, whereas our entire body is totally dependent on the mind for its health and well-being.

The body may influence the behaviors of our mind, but it is the mind that controls the body. This realization regarding the relationship between body and

mind led the masters of yoga to discover and awaken
the infinite potentials that normally lie dormant in
the mind. That is why yogis proclaim that the mind is
at the center of human existence. Upon knowing the
mind, everything is known. Upon gaining access to
your own mind, you gain access to everything there
is. Upon gaining victory over the mind, you are vic-
torious in every aspect of life. Self-realization, practi-
cally speaking, means the understanding of your
mind. The set of practices that enables you to gain
this self-realization and attain the perennial joy is
called yoga.

Yoga is the path of self-discipline, self-mastery, and
self-realization. It makes you understand who you
are, where you have come from, what the purpose of
life is, how you can make the best use of all the
resources you have, and, ultimately, how to live a joyful, productive, and peaceful life. The goal of this
path is to know yourself at every level—learn who you
are at the level of your body, breath, mind, and consciousness. While practicing yoga, you will come to
know the dynamics of body and mind, and how both
the body and mind are linked together with a life
force known as prana. Yogic practices can help you
provide complete rest to your body and attain a tranquil state of mind, which is necessary for attaining
success both in your worldly as well as in your spiritual endeavors.

No matter whether you are from the East or the West, whether you are a man or a woman, whether you are young or old, rich or poor, you need a healthy body and a sound mind to move forward on the path and reach your destination. A healthy body and a sound mind are as great necessities to Americans as they are to the Chinese, Japanese, or to anyone else. Yoga offers you the tools and means to take your health and happiness to the next level, provided you practice the ancient wisdom of yoga properly. Then definitely you can have a vibrant body and joyful mind and attain the highest goal of life: self-realization in this very lifetime.

The word *yoga* is derived from the verb *yuj*, which means to unite, to combine, to link, to join, to re-establish a state of balance and harmony. It is the path of integration and union. This integration and union refers to every aspect of our being. By practicing yoga, you balance your brain and your heart. You create an environment wherein the different systems of your body not only function well, but also support each other's functions.

If you are a medical practitioner, you will know that there is a close relationship between the functions of your lungs and heart, heart and brain, and liver and digestive system. There is a very close relationship between your respiratory and circulatory systems. You can clearly see how problems in your colon affect your stomach. These relationships indicate that in order to insure your health, you have to pay attention to all the limbs and organs of your body. Yogic practices require you to work with your entire body. You unfold the potentials of your body from inside out and make the best use of the resources that lie in the external world to support, heal, and nourish the forces that work inside you. This is called the process of integration and union. This set of practices, which evolved in the East over the centuries and can help you perfect the process of integration and union, came to be known as yoga.

The next level of yoga teaches us how to create a harmonious balance between our body and mind. Before we try to establish a state of balance between body and mind, we have to understand the dynamics of the mind—its nature, its intrinsic qualities and attributes, and how the mind rules over matter. Proper understanding of the mind is crucial in the process of yoga. That is why, in ancient times, yoga was defined as the path that leads to the mastery over the modifications of the mind. The classical system of yoga, also known as raja yoga, teaches us how emotions influence our physiology and biochemistry. It also teaches us how and why emotions originate, how to get into the bottom of the lake of the mind, and how to gain direct experience of the inner functionings of the mind and attain mastery over all of its aspects.

Then comes the next step of yoga. At this stage, we learn not only how to integrate the forces of body and mind, but also how to use all the forces of body and mind to serve the purpose of the soul. This is where yoga offers tools and means that can be used to explore and find the true meaning and purpose of life. This is where we learn the art of performing our actions skillfully and wisely. This is where we learn to form the philosophy of life that enables us to remain unperturbed in the face of all situations and circumstances. This level of yogic philosophy helps us to work hard, be productive, and enjoy our success with perfect equanimity.

Quite often, people become so excited when met with success that they are no longer able to enjoy their achievement. A student of yoga knows how to enjoy all the objects of the world and yet remain above the world. This philosophy also helps you to maintain your equanimity when you are met with failure. A real successful person is he or she whose happiness is not affected by success and failure, loss and gain, and honor and insult. Yogic philosophy leads you to that level of success. Actual practice to apply that philosophy in your daily life is called yoga *sadhana*.

Then comes the final stage of integration and union. Here you learn not only how to use your physical and mental resources to serve the purpose of the soul, but also how to offer your spiritual wealth at the

feet of the Divine Being. At this stage, you understand that no matter how successful you are on this
material plane and in the spiritual realm, you are still
a tiny spark, and that spark must shine in its fullness
and one day become one with the Absolute Divine
Being whose light illuminates the entire world from
eternity to eternity. Here the yoga that emphasizes
self-effort turns into the path of self-surrender. It is
on the path of self-surrender that you aspire to merge
with the Lord of Life.

For all practical purposes, the mind is at the core of
yoga philosophy. Similarly, the techniques that help
us organize all the faculties of mind make the mind
one-pointed, purified, focused, and ultimately unleashes
the indomitable will, inner strength, and the power
of intuition that are at the core of yoga practices.
The mind is the best tool that nature has given us.
By using this tool, we can discover the limitless
wealth that lies in this world and the boundless joy
that is buried within us. But if the mind itself is dull,
scattered, disoriented, and disheartened, we are lost.
That is why the wise say, "A confused mind is not
fit to follow any path." A confused mind robs us of
our purity of heart. A confused mind contaminates
our loving relationship. A confused mind distorts our
perception of ourselves and others, creates conflict
within and without, and then runs frantically to find a
solution to its self-created misery.

The mind stands between this world and ourselves and between ourselves and God. If the mind is clear, stable, friendly, honest, and well intentioned, then we gain a true understanding of the world and a true understanding of the reality within us. All the obstacles, conflicts, and misunderstandings vanish in a flash. We will have a healthy relationship with ourselves and a healthy relationship with others. We'll have a natural love and respect for ourselves and for others. Under no circumstance will we see life as a punishment. We'll adore it as a gift from the Divine. A spontaneous and long-lasting process of transformation within and without will emerge. The perennial joy that springs from the core of our being will begin to nourish all aspects of our existence. Then not only we, but all those near and dear to us, will begin to bask in the joyful and vibrant energy that radiates from the core of our being. Once you are blessed with a joyful mind, life is no longer a series of complicated events. You will be spontaneous in your thoughts, speech, and actions. Simplicity and spontaneity will become your nature.

These days, our lives are governed by science and technology. We are living in the age of machines. Science and technology have given us all kinds of comforts and conveniences, but lacking a right perspective in life, we are misusing and abusing them. Modern societies are obsessed by power. People are spending most of their time discovering the tools and means to become more powerful. Today, this hunger for power has led humanity toward self-destruction.

If you look at human civilization, you will find that technology has made great progress, but human beings have not progressed at all. In terms of inner development, we are standing at the same place where our forefathers stood in the Stone Age. The only progress that has been made is that in the olden days, people used to fight with sticks and pebbles and today, we fight with machine guns and nuclear weapons. We have learned how to harness atomic energy, but we have not yet learned how to manage our own senses and mind so that we can give a right direction to the energy that we gather in the external world. No matter how many international societies we form, and no matter how many peace summits we hold, unless we unveil the mysteries of the mind, we will continue using external forces to create misery for ourselves.

Today, so much energy is being channeled toward the external world. The modern system of education is designed to harness our mental and intellectual energy so that we accumulate more and more material objects. This is what modern people call evolution, growth, or progress. According to the ancients, this is called living an aimless life. In reality, very little evolution has taken place in our inner world. Our instincts, urges, passions, emotions, thoughts, and actions are as primitive today as they were in less so-called "advanced" ages. In fact, in terms of spiritual development, the human race has slid backward. There is more restlessness today than ever before. Violence, strife, discord, and the drive for sense pleasure are stronger than ever, too.

Great cultures such as those of ancient Egypt, Greece, China, and Rome tell us that power, position, and wealth are temporary phases that any civilization goes through. Real happiness does not depend on power, position, or material wealth; yet the lessons of history escape us. If you truly wish to find happiness here and now, study your mind and see how, normally, it is conditioned by time, space, and causation. The more desires you have, the more dissatisfaction you will have. However, it does not mean that you shun your will, becoming inert and useless to yourself and to others.

Great sages advise you to perform your actions skillfully, wisely, and lovingly. But make sure that you do not fall into the traps of your confused mind. Remember that most of the pleasures in the world are contaminated by fear and worry. If you do not understand that happiness is a creation of your mind, whereas experience of pleasure is an attribute of your senses, then definitely you will keep running after sense pleasures, and those sense pleasures will consume you.

Discipline your mind and sharpen your intellect so
that you can learn the techniques to make your body
and senses healthy and strong, so that you can enjoy
sense pleasures while remaining healthy and strong.
With a healthy body and a fulfilled mind, you'll be
able to understand the true nature of pleasure. This
understanding will lead you to see the distinction
between pleasure and happiness. This direct realization will help you long for everlasting happiness without being deprived of all the gifts that the body, senses,
and mind offer. This is what we learn and achieve by
practicing yoga and meditation.

A happy mind is the source of all healing powers. A
person with a happy mind is full of enthusiasm,
courage, and self-motivation. A person with a happy
mind is free from all complaints. Cultivating a joyful
mind is the greatest of all spiritual practices. All
human beings, regardless of whether they come from
the East or the West, are equally in need of happiness.
According to the yogis, happiness is always preceded
by peace. A quiet mind is the foundation for cultivating
a joyful mind. Mental quietude depends on one of the
greatest virtues: inner purity. Without inner purity,
we suffer from inner poverty. The whole process of
yoga, therefore, is an ascent into the purity that leads
to quietude of mind.

From a practical standpoint, the removal of impurities

is the way to cultivate inner purity. Anger, hatred, jealousy, greed, insatiable desire, attachment, and ego pollute our mind. These mental pollutants instigate our subhuman tendencies, thoughts, and feelings. Once these subhuman tendencies take over, we begin to behave like animals. Our inner balance and harmony are lost. Yoga is the way to re-establish our inner balance and harmony because it removes the impurities that churn and grind our higher virtues. That is why, in addition to delineating the yogic techniques for working with the body and mind, yoga offers ethical and moral guidelines for bringing the sacred into the mundane and creating a bridge between our outer and inner worlds. Unless we understand what those ethical and moral guidelines are, and unless we apply them in our daily life, the mere practice of yoga remains mechanical, dry, and spiritually speaking, lifeless.

The greatest mystery, as I mentioned earlier, lies in the depths of the mind itself. In fact, the mind itself is a great mystery. No matter what kind of yoga you practice, no matter at what level of yoga you practice, the mind is the first and foremost tool that you can use. If this tool itself is faulty, you cannot reach your destination safely. If the mind is purified, it can become a great friend in your journey. If it is impure, unstable, and noisy, it can also become your worst enemy. Normally, people living in the world have a restless mind. If they wish to be successful in their worldly endeavors or spiritual practice, they first have to overcome mental restlessness and make their minds quiet, steady, and peaceful. Then later, using this purified, steady, and quiet mind, they can explore both the outer and inner world and enjoy life in its fullest.

Why is the mind restless? Because our minds and hearts are filled with endless desires. We hardly pause to ponder how many of those desires are good, constructive, and healthy for us. Without paying attention to the objects of desire, and without caring whether or not they are worth paying attention to, we run after those desires. Those who run after desires without weighing all the pros and cons lack insight. Their lives are consumed by their desires, and such people have no time and energy to explore and find meaning and purpose in life. Since they do not know why they are running after the objects of desire, when they achieve their desired object, they find no satisfaction and thus they go on blindly chasing one desire after another. In the process, they get exhausted. Their willpower weakens. Their power of discrimination declines. They lose control over their mind. And they become a complete victim of their desires. In order to live a happy and healthy life, therefore, you must evaluate your desires and go after only such desires that are useful, healthy, and conducive to your journey. But you can do it only when you learn to quiet down your mind, and with a quiet mind, contemplate on the higher meaning and purpose of life.

In search of a quiet mind, you do not need to renounce your home. You do not need to abandon your worldly duties and obligations. You do not need to retire from your job and lock yourself in a cave. All you need to do is to simplify your life and learn the art of performing your duties skillfully and wisely, selflessly and lovingly; learn to perform your actions without being attached to the fruits of your actions.

Religionists all over the world have created an unnecessary confusion regarding spirituality and the freedom of spirit. Yoga does not encourage a monastic life. Through the practice of yoga, you unveil the mystery of your mind and the vast universe that is created and sustained by the mind. By practicing yoga, you unveil the mysteries of the mind layer by layer. Finally, you reach that center of tranquility where you can listen to the eternal song spontaneously sung by the Divine within you. From the core of that quietude, you bring that music into the outer layers of your being and infuse your total well-being with that inner music. This is what will enable you to make your mind become steady and one-pointed. This will also help your body and senses to hear and heed the voice of your soul. Thus, the practice of non-attachment and of performing your actions selflessly and lovingly is the way to quiet your mind, purify it, and make it steady.

To many beginner students, the idea of non-attachment and practicing dispassion may sound difficult. Many people in the world suffer from such poor health that they have neither time nor energy to even think about whether their desires and attachments have anything to do with their pain and misery. In such a case, good health, a sound mind, as well as a desire to live, be happy, and be fulfilled in life are necessary requirements. Their journey must begin from a point that ensures good health. Restoring good health in such situations is even more important than dealing with the mind. To progress on the path of health and happiness, people must learn how to eat, sleep, exercise, relax, and rest. They must learn how purity of food leads to purity of mind, and how heavy food leads to inertia. Similarly, techniques that ensure how to sleep well and not waste time tossing and turning and exhausting their energy in dreams are of utmost importance.

In the search for peace and happiness, the biggest mistake people make is that they ignore seven golden laws of healthy living. These basic principles are how to eat properly, how to breathe properly, how to sleep properly, how to think properly, how to enjoy sense pleasures properly, how to interact with others properly, and how to stay focused on the higher goal and purpose of life. Unless you comply with these seven golden laws, you will continue to struggle with your personal, family, professional, and social life. No matter how smart and intelligent you are, you will remain a victim of sloth and inertia. Despite your intentions to live a productive life, you will suffer from a lack of stamina. You will end up with a weak body and a scattered mind. You will waste time fighting with a long chain of obstacles arising from your unhealthy body and restless mind. There will be very little time and energy left for working toward your main goal, be it worldly or spiritual. The removal of obstacles, therefore, is even more important than working toward your main goal. That is why compliance with these seven golden laws helps you prepare the foundation for living a joyful life.

Upon realizing the fact that human beings have formed the habit of leaning on others, the great adepts chalked out an entire plan for mastering the art of joyful living in eight simple and systematic steps. Those eight steps, known as raja yoga, automatically include the seven golden laws mentioned above as well as the actual methodical practice to unfold all the potentials that lie dormant in our body, mind, and soul, the center of consciousness within.

The first step toward mastering the art of joyful living in yoga is known as *yama*—self-regulation, self-observation. The word *yama* literally means "that which helps us stay within our boundaries and not trespass others' boundaries." In modern language, it means to "live and let live." At this step, we try to understand and embrace the five principles of non-violence, truthfulness, non-stealing, non-indulgence, and non-possessiveness. Non-violence means be nice to yourself and be nice to others. Truthfulness means be honest with yourself and be honest with others. Non-stealing means refrain from usurping that which is not yours and be happy with that which is lawfully yours. Non-indulgence means do not misuse or abuse your body, senses, and mind. Enjoy all the gifts that nature has given you but only in a manner that nourishes your body and mind without draining the sap of life, the vitality that you need to complete your life's journey. Non-possessiveness means do not hold physical and emotional objects to the point where your house, your body, your senses, and your mind turn into a junkyard. This five-fold practice of yama, self-observance, helps you simplify your life. By practicing these five observances, you will no longer be a source of threat to anybody. People will be comfortable with you; and, of course, you will no longer be a source of threat to yourself, so definitely you will be at peace with yourself.

The second step in the practice of yoga is known as *niyama*, which literally means "self-discipline and self-commitment." This step also consists of five components: cleanliness, contentment, "austerity," self-study, and surrender to God. While practicing niyama, all you have to do is be clean and straight-forward in your thoughts, speech, and actions. Let there be cleanliness in the world outside you and purity in the world inside you. Work as hard as you wish. Set as high a goal as you wish. But be content with the fruits of your actions. This contentment, however, does not mean that you become complacent or fall into the trap of inertia and inactivity. It simply means perform your actions without suffering from the fever of anxiety. Commit yourself to *tapas*, which is literally translated as "austerity." The actual meaning of *tapas*, however, is adopting a lifestyle where you begin to shine in your thoughts, speech, and actions. Adopt a lifestyle where you become a light to yourself and a light to others. You commit yourself to self-study. Self-study means you study your body, mind, and senses. You study your thoughts, speech, and actions. You study your habit patterns, and you study your strengths and weaknesses. Through self-study, you gain a right understanding of yourself as well as the world both outside of you and inside of you. Finally, you infuse your life with the presence of the Divine. This is called surrender to God. In the yogic tradition, the practice of surrendering yourself to God does not require any ritual or ceremonial paraphernalia. Surrender to God means that you remain aware of the Divine being, the Lord of Life within you, and in all situations and circumstances. you remind yourself that the Lord of the Universe, the most compassionate Divine Being, is always with you. She is the source of true life.

These first two steps of yoga constitute the moral and ethical aspects of yoga philosophy and practice. Unless you embrace the five principles of self-observance and the five principles of self-discipline, your entire endeavor—both worldly and spiritual—will constantly be impeded by endless obstacles. Unless you apply these principles, you will find yourself an alien while living in a family and in a society. Without these principles, any practice that you undertake for your spiritual unfoldment and total well-being will be like a body without breath.

The third step of the practice is called *asana*, the postures. After hundreds of years of constant research and personal practice, yogis in the East concluded that the human body is endowed with limitless potentials. The body is equipped with all the reasons to make itself sick, and the body is equipped with all the forces to heal itself. It is totally up to us whether we want to live with an unhealthy body or a vibrant body. Adepts have discovered eighty-four classical postures, with endless variations and derivatives, that can help us ensure a vibrant body wherein the soul can carry a joyful mind. All the postures, for the sake of study, can be classified into two main categories: physical postures and meditative postures. Physical postures have a direct impact on restoring physical health and an indirect impact on cultivating a joyful mind. Meditative postures, on the other hand, have a direct impact on cultivating a joyful mind, and an indirect impact on restoring physical health.

The fourth step is known as *pranayama*. *Prana* means "life force;" *ayama* means "expansion." Together, they mean practices that help us infuse our body and mind with vital energy, the life force. These practices consist of breathing exercises. Breathing exercises are more subtle and more potent than the practice of postures. By using the techniques of breathing exercises, you can strengthen and revitalize the internal organs in the body, nourish the senses, heal emotional injuries, and nurture the mind. Since the practice of pranayama is more subtle and potent, it requires greater precaution. Preparation for the practice of pranayama is much more sophisticated than the practice of postures. In the practice of pranayama, you make sure that your diet is balanced and the air you breathe is fresh and clean. There are also guidelines that you may use to determine whether or not you are practicing your breathing exercises correctly, making sure that you stay within your limits and expand your capacity in a safe and gradual manner.

Then comes the fifth step, which in the yogic tradition is known as *pratyahara*. The word *pratyahara* literally means to disentangle yourself wisely and skillfully. Quite often in English this word is translated as "sense withdrawal." That frightens Western students. But when you analyze the meaning of this word, with each of its prefixes and verb, then you realize that this particular step of yoga refers to a very crucial stage in the journey of life. The prefix *prati*, means to pull yourself from an undesirable point in time and space and unite yourself with that which is useful and desirable. The other prefix, *a*, means from every direction, in every respect. The word *hara* is derived from the verb root *hri*, that is, to carry, to lead, to guide, to supervise. Together, both prefixes and the verb mean to disentangle our senses and mind from the unhealthy and undesirable objects of the world, gather all the scattered pieces of the mind, and turn them inward to explore the higher dimensions of life.

The practice of the fifth step of yoga is a natural evolution in the soul's journey. When we find ourselves standing at a crossroad, we run from one object to another, from one job to another, from one career to another, from one relationship to another. At some point, we find ourselves exhausted. Our hearts demand that our mind clarify the purpose behind this endless race. That is when, whether you are interested in the practice of yoga or not, you end up re-evaluating the meaning and purpose of life. This re-evaluation motivates you to pause for a while and see whether this non-stop and almost purposeless marathon race for the charms and temptations of the world is worth-while. Every human being, at some point in life, finds himself standing at this crossroad. The decision to withdraw himself from the alluring sights that line the roads and to drive only on the road that makes the most sense is called *pratyahara*, which in part refers to "sense withdrawal," but in part also refers to turning the mind inward.

The sixth step is *dharana*, concentration. This is where you truly learn to gather all the forces and the faculties of the mind, focusing them on one chosen object. Nowhere else will you find such a well-developed system to cultivate your retentive power than in yoga. The most important component in the practice of concentration is the selection of the object of concentration. You can focus your mind on an external object or an internal one. It is advised that this process of selecting an object be done by someone who knows all the qualities and attributes of the object of concentration, because over a period of time, as you continue concentrating on an object, the mind begins to absorb all of the object's qualities and characteristics. The object of concentration, therefore, must be accompanied by uplifting energies. Only then will you see a qualitative change taking place in yourself.

The seventh step is meditation, which in the yoga tradition is known as *dhyana*. Meditation is simply an advanced stage of concentration. Concentration makes the mind one-pointed and steady, whereas in meditation, it begins to expand and to touch the dimension of reality, which is known as the field of intuition. A meditator gains a level of clarity of mind that is not to be found in an ordinary situation. Even in this state, however, a meditator is not fully established in his essential nature. He may be getting glimpses of a higher level of reality and yet he is still aware of the lower level of reality. Through constant practice, the meditative experience becomes more refined, and one day there emerges a pure and perfect state of spiritual absorption known as *samadhi*, the eighth and final stage in the practice of yoga.

In the highest state of yogic accomplishment, you are fully at peace. You are perfectly established in supreme consciousness. The experience of equanimity you gain at this stage cannot be compared with anything. It is indescribable. The experience of bliss is not outside you; it is inside you and it is you. There is no sense of duality in this state. You are in the world and the world is in you. You are in God and God is in you. You have transcended your mind and the realm of consciousness that is limited by time, space, and causation. There is no distinction between the past, present, and future. The world known by the senses and the world beyond the reach of the senses are fully integrated in this spiritually illumined consciousness. Upon reaching this state, you have not only known the meaning of life, but also you have found it. All your desires and cravings have been fulfilled, for you have found your eternal friend, your inner soul, and thus you are no longer lonely. Freedom from loneliness allows the descent of such a powerful peace and joy that you long for nothing anymore. This is called attaining perfection and attaining immortality. Upon experiencing this level of joy, you begin to see the whole world filled with an indescribable beauty and joy. Regardless of whether you are young or old, man or woman, you find yourself beautiful. This experience of being a beautiful person is so real and fulfilling that you do not need others to admire your beauty. Rather, you find yourself brimming with the joy that your inner beauty is beyond all admiration. That is how this eight-step yoga helps you master the art of joyful living and guarantees that you will find meaning and purpose in life here and now. This path is so profound and yet so simple that anyone from any level of physical capacity, emotional maturity, intellectual grasp, and philosophical and cultural background can follow this path. This system of yoga is called raja yoga, the royal path.

Chapter Two

Cultivating a Quiet Mind

THE PEOPLE OF THE MODERN WORLD ARE mesmerized by science and technology. Our industrial output makes us believe that today we are more prosperous and fortunate than our ancestors. We are very proud of our comforts and conveniences, and we have a genuine reason to give credit to science and technology for all of our achievements. But few of us pay attention to the fact that the unprecedented progress in the external world has not brought us closer to our home—the real home—where we can pause for a moment and rest, reflect, renew, and enjoy our worldly achievements. I see people running amuck. I feel pity for the modern system of education, which enforces the idea that the more we know about the external world, the wiser and more learned we will become. It saddens me to see modern men measuring success by the acquisition of worldly objects. I can also, however, see why. People in every part of the world today look up to the Western culture and its values, ideas, and lifestyle. The Western culture derives its worldview from a philosophy that seeks fulfillment in an ever-expanding possessiveness and ownership of as many objects as possible.

Western philosophy explores and examines the material world. The purpose behind this exploration is normally to conquer and consume, possess, and gain exclusive ownership. This forces a human being to identify himself with objects of the world. This identification alienates him from his inner self. Not having the inner self as an anchor, a person goes on drifting from one wave of fear to another wave of doubt. Anxiety and insecurity grip his mind. Eastern philosophy, which today is often subdued by the Western way of thinking, focuses on exploring the subtle-most aspects of human existence. Eastern philosophy explores and examines the inner dimensions of life. The purpose behind a person's inner discovery is to find the ultimate truth and extricate himself from inner turmoil. In theory, people in the East should be at greater peace and more grounded; but upon observing, I find that people, both in the East and the West, are confronted with the same fate—lack of contentment, peace, and happiness.

People everywhere have the same emotions. They share similar tendencies. The desire to enjoy life and live joyfully is common to all human beings. It is this desire that compels us to undertake all of our worldly and spiritual endeavors. At the onset of any endeavor, we must realize that success depends on how grounded we are within ourselves. Without a calm and tranquil mind, we can be successful neither in the material world nor our spiritual world. We must learn the art of acquiring a quiet mind. To meet this challenge, there is no better tool than meditation, for meditation alone enables us to know ourselves at every level. Meditation alone enables us to create a bridge between different aspects of our being—between body and breath, between breath and mind, and between mind and soul.

From our early childhood, we are taught to examine and verify things in the external world. No one teaches us how to know ourselves. And unless we know ourselves, we cannot understand our true relationship with others. Without this understanding, we go on forming and dismantling one relationship after another, getting hurt in the process. By the time we become an adult, our life is a catalog of emotional injuries. Each injury contributes to the next level of mistrust, doubt, and fear. We go on seeking a cure to life's problems in the external world without much success. In our modern society, we do not find any examples from which we can learn how to turn our attention inward and search for the cure inside. Our inability to turn our mind inward forces us to live under stress and strain.

You are very successful in the external world, but what good is that success if you have not found peace within? You are hungry and a beautiful platter of food is before you; however, your hands are tied and you are not able to pick up the food and put it in your mouth. What is the use of that food? Untie yourself first; only then will you enjoy what you have. Conquer the roaming tendencies of your mind. Disentangle it from its self-created distractions. Release it from the charms and temptations of the world so that it can come back to its abode, which is you. Only then can it attend to the core of your being, the center of peace and tranquility. This is called meditation.

Many Christians say that there is no mention of meditation in the Bible; therefore, meditation is not compatible with Christianity. It surprises me how the Bible scholars don't see written so clearly, "Be still and know that I am God." What a wonderful verse. If you learn to be still, you will not have to listen to

Swami Rama. Your own still mind will reveal the true content and intent of your beautiful scripture. Your stillness will tell you how God resides in the innermost chamber of your heart, and how your heart goes on playing the divine music perennially.

The Divine Being resides at the lotus of the heart. All we need to do is turn our mind and see the blossoming of that heart. All great scriptures of the world say in one voice, "The Lord of Life, the Divine Being, is all-pervading, eternal, without beginning or end." The Divine Being is far away from those who lack a calm and tranquil mind and very close to those who have a tranquil mind and can sit still. Mental stillness comes through meditation.

People sometimes ask me, "How can I live an active and productive life if I become still due to the practice of meditation? The world out there demands that I run faster than everyone else in order to win the race. I am afraid that meditation might take competitiveness away from me." I remind such people that in order to live an active and productive life, you have to charge your body and mind with vitality and stamina. Meditation will help you replenish your body on a daily basis. It helps you calm down your nervous system; it helps you relax your muscles and thus release the tension that you hold in your body. Look at the medical data about how tension leads to coronary problems and nervous breakdowns—not to mention ulcers, dyspepsia, hypertension, and many other ailments. Meditation will help you organize your mind and think in a linear and structured manner. It will boost your memory; it will sharpen your intellect. To accomplish a task, worldly or spiritual, you need a clear mind and a sharp intellect. It's the one-pointed mind that enables you to think, analyze, decide, and act. And it is meditation that helps you cultivate such a one-pointed mind.

Meditation doesn't make you inert; rather, it makes you active, as well as grounded. Due to the tranquility that you gain through meditation, you are no longer the victim of any form of agitation. A person with an unsettled mind complains, "My husband is not behaving properly—that is why I am suffering." The husband insists, "My wife does not do her job—that is why I am suffering." All domestic disputes have their roots in agitated minds. If you want to create a peaceful and joyful atmosphere in your family, society, and nation, you had best learn the art of acquiring a peaceful mind. Inner tranquility will infuse your atmosphere, your outer world, with patience, fortitude, and tolerance. It will help you cultivate sensitivity toward others. You will become a kind, loving person. Your productivity will soar because you will have fewer obstacles to face.

A person with an unclear and disturbed mind has no choice but to go on blaming others for his misery. No one wants to be blamed for others' faults. Therefore, a complainer is always left in isolation. Such a complainer becomes a victim of his distorted perception that everyone is after him. He becomes defensive, for he sees others as his enemies. Negativity grips him. His relationships become inflicted with loneliness. The cure for this loneliness, therefore, is to repair your mind—make it positive, turn it inward, and reflect within. While standing on the firm foundation of a tranquil mind, examine the cause of your loneliness. You can build this firm foundation only through meditation.

Meditation is the best tool with which to study yourself—your body, mind, and consciousness. On the path of meditation, first become aware of your body. You realize the importance of having a good, healthy body. Your personal experience will tell you that you can only contain a sound mind in a healthy body. This realization will lead you to look after your diet and be energetic. That is why the ancient masters included the guidelines for maintaining physical health in their regimen. They knew that an undernourished body would become a source of mental and emotional hunger. A body filled with toxins contributes to mental impurity. Knowing the intricate relationship between body and mind, the ancient masters taught how to maintain a harmonious balance between the two. That is how they developed the system of raja yoga—the most balanced, holistic path to spiritual unfoldment and total well-being.

You are a human being. Within you resides God and all Godly powers. You are a direct manifestation of that Godly power. You are blessed with infinite potential. Due to carelessness, most of that potential remains dormant. The purpose of human birth is to awaken that potential. You have been blessed with the capacity to awaken it. How precious is human birth. Human beings are perhaps the only creatures with the privilege to stand against the laws of nature. Unlike other animals, you can regulate your urges. You don't have to wait for a particular season to procreate. Look at your body—your bones and ligaments allow you to stand in a way that fights the pull of gravity. No other creatures can arrange their extremities as you can. No other creature can regulate its breath as you can. No other creature can relax voluntarily as you can. The more you understand your body, the more your heart becomes filled with gratitude to the Creator. This natural unfoldment of gratitude is the beginning of your unconditional love for God. The day you learn to sit, breathe, and relax in a manner conducive to your inner journey, you become a yogi—the seeker of your hidden wealth.

As a seeker, first learn to sit comfortably. A posture in which your spine is straight, shoulders relaxed, and the weight of your body equally distributed on your buttocks is called a yogic posture. As part of your inward journey, simply learn to sit quietly for a while. Physical comfort and stillness is a prerequisite to cultivating a quiet mind. Allow a couple months just to perfect a sitting posture. It is not necessary for you to twist your legs, ending up at the doctor's office. If you cannot sit in a comfortable, cross-legged posture, then you can use a chair. Sitting on a chair is also a yoga posture, called *maitri-asana*, the friendship pose. The important thing, however, is that you sit with your head, neck, and trunk in a straight line.

When you are trying to gain physical stillness by sitting in a meditative pose, make sure that you pay attention to your breath. Breathe gently and smoothly. There should not be any jerk, noise, or shakiness in your breath. The more attention you pay to your breath, the more comfortable you will be in your sitting pose. But if you are not sitting properly, then it will be hard for you to eliminate the jerk, noise, and shallowness from your breath. That is how you can start your inward journey—by first learning how to sit comfortably.

Medical science has just begun discovering that most diseases are psychosomatic. Most often, the seeds of diseases that manifest in our bodies are found in our minds. But just because we do not know exactly how the body and mind relate and interact, we fail to understand how these diseases, deposited deep in our mind field, manifest in our bodies. The scriptures, such as the Upanishads and *Yoga Sutra*, explain this body-mind relationship. These texts describe in great detail the dynamics of the mind and its modifications. There we find how our thoughts affect our nervous system, how our emotions influence the functions of our endocrine system, and how much impact our positive and negative thoughts have on our heart. The entire study of the body-mind relationship concludes that it is the breath that holds together, as well as nourishes, both our body and mind. Breath is the key to our physical and mental health and well-being.

So, let us examine what the breath is. How do we breathe? And what do we gain beyond the intake of oxygen and the output of carbon dioxide? According to yoga scriptures, the breath is the protector of the City of Life. Two guards—inhalation and exhalation—are constantly guarding the city that you call the body. Even when you sleep, they remain awake. They are constantly working for you.

Let us look at the anatomy of breathing. Normally, you fill your lungs with air when you inhale and your lungs unload the carbon dioxide as you exhale. Breath is paramount to providing fresh energy from the atmosphere and eliminating toxins from the body. The role of the breath in maintaining physical health and in keeping us alive is known to the medical world. But modern science knows little or even nothing about the breath's role in maintaining our mental health.

Understanding the relationship between breathing and the functions of the mind is central to the study of yoga. According to the yogis, only after learning something about your breathing do you begin to understand how your conscious mind functions. In our modern system of education, we have learned how to train our conscious mind so that we gather and deposit information and become skilled professionals. The modern system of education, however, does not pay any attention to how to nourish and make this mind vibrant and active. The result is that today many people suffer from mental overload. Even people in their early youth and teens carry heavy and hazy heads. Upon seeing them, my heart hurts. I wonder, what is wrong with people? Why can't they can't fix this problem, which is so simple?

By learning some simple breathing techniques, these people can energize their brains and nervous systems, throw away their mental burdens, clear their minds, and sharpen their intellects. But instead, people go on living with this mental impoverishment until one day the whole system crashes. Then they seek the cure in the external world—counseling, psychotherapy, and heavy drugs. According to the yogis, living in this condition means letting outside forces run your most private world—the mind. There cannot be a greater slavery than letting someone else manage your mind. A person who has leased his mind to someone else can never be happy. Therefore, you had better take charge of your mind; be master of your mind; be creator of your destiny. You can do it when you know how to breathe properly.

When I first came to this country, I couldn't understand why when people were walking they were holding so much tension in their shoulders. In cities like New York and Detroit, it looked as though even the elements were filled with stress. You could feel stress in the air. I wondered why I saw beautiful buildings, huge stores, fancy cars, people making lots of money, and yet it seemed that their shoulders were not able to carry the burden of their heads. As I paid attention, I realized that most people did not breathe properly. I was shocked to see that the most important part of the body involved in the breathing process was almost frozen. Do you know what that is? It is the diaphragm—the muscle that, when it contracts, presses against your lungs, forcing air out, and as it relaxes, allows the lungs to expand, thus pulling air in. I saw people living on "chest breathing," and I found that unnatural and unscientific.

Back in the Himalayas, my master and other adepts had taught me that only by breathing deeply and smoothly without jerks, noises, or pauses, can you regulate the functions of your internal organs as well as the functions of your mind. I was taught that by breathing diaphragmatically, I could relax my nervous system, revitalize my organs, and energize my brain cells. I was taught that by breathing diaphragmatically, I could regulate my thinking process, strengthen my memory, and provide such a deep level of rest to both my body and mind that I could reduce my dream cycles. By applying proper methods of breathing, I could enter a deep sleep in which the mind could find the most profound rest, and thus, I did not have to waste my night tossing and turning, dreaming and snoring. But here, it was rare to find people breathing in a healthy way. That made me understand why such a large percentage of the population in the United States is clinically diagnosed with schizophrenia.

Why are people irritable? Why do they lose their tempers so easily? Why has their forbearance declined? The answer is simple—their minds, and the energy channels through which they travel, are undernourished. If you learn the proper method of breathing, you can rejuvenate your mind. You will see how the mind's inherent virtues—such as patience, fortitude, and willpower—rise. That is why proper breathing is such an essential part of the practice of meditation.

On the path to cultivate a quiet mind, you start exactly where you stand. Most of the time, you exist at the level of your body consciousness. Most of your concerns are related to the needs and demands, comforts and conveniences of your body. Therefore, you must first learn the fundamental principles of maintaining a good, healthy body. You can restore and maintain a healthy body by eating the right food. A fresh, nutritious, light meal, at the right time, in the right proportion, and with the right attitude lies at the core of a healthy diet. You don't have to become a diet maniac; all you have to do is see what and how much you must eat to supply only the amount of nutrients your body needs. Even the most nutritious food eaten disproportionately becomes a source of disease. Food should not be undercooked or overcooked. Whole grains accompanied by fresh vegetables are always good. From the beginning of human civilization, people have included dairy in their diet. Any allergy to milk products is a sign and symptom of your inner imbalance. That needs to be cured rather than discarding the dairy itself.

Good health also requires that you exercise daily. Exercises that keep your cardiovascular system active and healthy are of utmost importance. The most scientific and comprehensive system of exercise ever developed is hatha yoga. No exercise can revitalize every limb, organ, and system of the body as efficiently and profoundly as hatha yoga. I am talking about the authentic method of hatha yoga as described in the ancient texts, such as the *Hatha Yoga Pradipika* and a number of the Upanishads.

Today, I see so many people teaching and practicing "yoga." Most of it, in my opinion, is a joke. Many of the subtleties of hatha yoga have been replaced with a fanciful turning and twisting of the body. I rarely see modern teachers teaching pranayama, *kriyas*, and *mudras*. It is these components that distinguish hatha yoga from other systems of exercise. And it is these components that awaken the forces that normally remain dormant in the body. The practice of hatha yoga is not meant to burn calories; it is to make your body flexible and to strengthen your respiratory, circulatory, and nervous systems. It is to help you expand your stamina and boost your immune system. It is to detoxify your body and to nurture the organs that are constantly working to nourish your body and mind. I advise that you learn the discipline of hatha yoga from a competent teacher who can teach you something more than yoga postures. Postures form just the preliminary stage in the practice of yoga. Without the practice of pranayama, hatha yoga is not complete. Even this practice should be done in moderation.

Regularity lies at the foundation of any practice you do. People come to me saying, "Swamiji, I do not know what is wrong with my practice. I have been doing my yoga and meditation for so long, but I don't see very many results." When I ask them, "Do you practice daily?" normally the answer is, "I do it a few times a week, sometimes in the morning and sometimes in the evening." It doesn't work that way. A practice gives its result only when you do it systematically, regularly, and for a prolonged period of time. To assist your practice, form a habit of going to bed on time and waking up on time. Also form a habit of evacuating your system first thing in the morning. Bring the practice of hatha yoga and meditation into your daily routine. Then you will see how your body and mind become a source of happiness.

Then comes meditation. These days, the word *meditation* is quite misused and misunderstood. Normally, people think that meditation means "emptying one's mind"; that is incorrect. You cannot empty your mind. The mind is not a physical entity that you can acquire, use, and dispose of at your pleasure. It is not a container that you can fill and empty at your wish. It is an energy field that is filled with thoughts, ideas, emotions, and sentiments. Most of these mental constructs spring from four primitive urges: fear, sleep, sex, and self-preservation. These primitive urges are common to all living beings. Human beings have been given a great degree of freedom to conquer, control, use, misuse, and even abuse these urges. Those who do not pay attention to the higher faculty within and who do not manage these urges wisely lose mastery over their minds, for these urges keep influencing the functions and behaviors of the mind.

Meditation allows you to still the mind, look at it objectively, and see which of the mental contents are useful and which are not. By watching the modifications of the mind and by looking at their source, you can clearly see what kind of impressions you have deposited in your mind field. By following the two-fold path of meditation—*abhyasa* (methodical practice) and *vairagya* (dispassion)—you can free your mind of unwanted, undesirable thoughts and emotions. That is how you eventually acquire a quiet mind. It is this quiet mind that can help you see yourself without any distortion. It is this quiet mind that can help you see the world without any distortion. You will have the right perspective of yourself and the outside world. Your understanding of yourself and your loved ones will help you have realistic expectations of your relationships with others. False expectations will fall away. Expectation is the mother of all frustrations and disappointments. Freedom from expectations becomes a source of happiness here and now.

— Chapter Three —

Unveiling the
Mystery of the Mind

I WAS BORN IN THE HIMALAYAS IN A FAMILY KNOWN for its knowledge of philosophy, spirituality, and the subjects documented in the scriptures. I became an orphan at an early age. My master, a saint from Bengal who lived in the Himalayas, adopted me as his own child. In addition to providing me with a regular education, he gave me lessons on the practical aspects of philosophy and spirituality. This gentle sage, whom I call my master, infused my heart with the desire to search for the True Self while I was still young. This desire led me to visit adepts who lived in the cave monasteries of the Himalayas. Regardless of where I went and whom I met, I heard one message again and again—the mind is the greatest of all mysteries. Upon unveiling this mystery, all mysteries are unveiled. As a young man, when I heard the adepts saying this, it made sense to me, but only intellectually. As I grew older, I understood the depth of that saying; and, finally, I concluded that unveiling the mystery of the mind lies at the core of every practice ever taught in every tradition.

Before I say more about the mystery of the mind, let me tell you something clearly and emphatically: the mind is the source of all misery and happiness. It is the source of both bondage and liberation. The more you know about your mind, the greater the mastery you will have over the world around you. When we talk about self-mastery, we are talking about mastery over the mind. No matter how educated you are, you can have control over yourself, others, and your circumstances only if you know something about the human mind. Today, there are departments in universities and colleges that specialize in such subjects as human development, cognitive psychology, and a variety of counseling techniques. So many business schools offer courses for developing leadership skills. Upon observation, I found that, by and large, all of these disciplines impart the skill to analyze and manipulate the thoughts and emotions of others to solve an issue at hand. What is missing in all of these systems of education is the understanding of the source of all the thoughts and emotions that create turmoil—first in our inner world, and then in the world outside us.

Modern scientists are trying to study the mind, but they are succeeding only in studying the brain. We have to clearly understand the distinction between the two. The mind is energy, but the brain is matter; it is only a vehicle of that energy. A scientific study of the physical brain cannot tell us much about the non-physical energy that is activating it.

Medical science tries to study the source of our thoughts and emotions, but only on the physical level. Modern scientists do not see a difference between the brain and the mind. In the name of studying the mental behaviors of a human being, they study the functions of the brain and neurological responses to external stimuli. Some study the mind from the standpoint of biochemistry. This particular branch of science seeks the source of our emotions and sentiments in the realm of our biochemistry. According to the science of yoga, this kind of study has nothing to do with the study of the mind. It is simply a study of the body—its limbs, its organs, its different systems, and how they interact with each other.

Yoga science affirms that the brain is a physical entity; it is made of matter. By itself, it is inert and aimless. Its function depends on the mind. By its volition, the mind shakes away the brain's inertia, sets an aim, and makes it function. The brain is like a computer's hardware. It is a raw machine. Its performance depends on the software. The mind is the programmer. The programmer has a goal and objectives. A programmer who does not know the exact goal cannot write a program precisely and successfully. He may work hard without getting anywhere, incurring unnecessary wear and tear on the hardware. So is the case with the mind.

There are many difficulties in the study of the mind. First, the mind is subtle; it is beyond the reach of physical instruments. Second, scientists are used to analyzing a subject in a lab, but the mind is not an aspect of our being that can be dissected, isolated, and analyzed for its constituents. Unlike any examples found in the external world, the mind alone, through its inwardly process, can look at itself and understand its behavior and the dynamics that enable it to function in unlimited ways. Therefore, we can know very little about our mind by analyzing the chemical components of our brain in a laboratory. We cannot know anything about our mind by organizing a debate about the dynamics of mind. To learn about the mind, we first have to enter our own mental domain. We have to turn our consciousness inward. We have to intuit our mind and all of its faculties directly. We have to gain a direct knowledge of how the mind functions and how it relates to the body, on one hand, and the soul, on the other. Through the eye of intuition, we have to see the force that breathes life into the mind, the force that provides nourishment to the mind. We have to cultivate penetrating eyesight to see beyond the physical sheath that we call the body. The technique that enables us to turn our focus inward, enter the inner realm, and see ourselves—our mind and all other inner faculties face to face—is called meditation. It is in the laboratory of meditation that we can unveil the mysteries of the mind. Only after we have discovered them can we understand the dynamics of our thoughts, feelings, and behaviors. This understanding can help us create a world both within and without that is conducive to our personal quest, peace, and happiness.

In India, when I reminded people about the importance of meditation, I got a flat response, "Oh, Swamiji, we are ordinary people—laymen. Meditation is for holy people like you." I heard others say, "We are householders. How can we meditate? We live in houses, not in caves. If I leave my home and go to the Himalayan caves, then who will take care of my business and my family? I don't want to run away from my duties and make the lives of others miserable. My salvation depends on your blessings."

It was very difficult to convince such people that you don't have to be known as a holy person in order to meditate. Holiness is not a prerequisite to meditation. Rather, the more you meditate, the holier you become. Meditation is the simple process of turning your mind inward. To do this, all you need is strong determination. With the power of determination, you gather the scattered pieces of your mind and pull them toward the core of your being, that is, the center of consciousness. Since, for a long time, the mind has formed a habit of chasing one object after another, you need to apply a systematic method to calm it down, and you have to convince it that there's a greater joy right within you. Once the mind understands that it does not need to wear itself down in order to find joy in the external world, it will easily come back to the core of your being. How you convince your mind of this fact requires that you form a philosophy of life, and how you actually bring it back to the core of your being requires that you employ a systematic method of meditation.

I conveyed this message to the people of India, but very few heard it. People visited me in large numbers because, in India, the culture imparts the belief that if you visit a swami, you will be blessed with health, wealth, progeny, and spiritual enlightenment. Visiting a "holy man" and getting a glance of him is called *darshan*, an act of spirituality believed to wash off all the impurities that you may have accumulated by living a normal life. Gathering around a holy man and listening to his discourses is called *satsang*, the basking in the company of a saint. Whenever I told such visitors and seekers that they should learn to take charge of their thoughts, speech, and actions, they would say, "Swamiji, I have put my soul at Thy feet. Why should I worry about anything now?" I felt sad for those people. I couldn't convince them that happiness lies within and that everyone has access to that happiness provided they make an effort.

In my sixty-five years of life, I could only teach the art of meditation to a few in India. Indian culture today is suffering from an addiction to guru worship and "personality cults." No medicine other than meditation can help people cure this addiction, for meditation enables a person to see that the divine light, the Divine Being that lies at the core of every individual, is the source of all the blessings that we mistakenly seek in the outside world. Thank God that Western culture does not believe in hero worship. I hope and I pray that the Western world refrains from falling victim to this addiction, a disease that kills the very spirit of freedom.

The Western world, however, has its own problem. Here, people are so engrossed in their bodies that they have a hard time seeing anything beyond this material plane. This has led them to place their trust only in what can be perceived through the senses and tested and verified through physical instruments. Despite so much progress in psychology, psychotherapy, and psychiatry, the research on mental diseases and mental health has not gone beyond the physical domain. Common sense and scientific evidence clearly point toward a non-physical realm as a source of our mental health and happiness; yet, the scientific community is refusing to acknowledge this fact. Why is that? In my opinion, it is fear of discovering something that was not known before. This tendency dominates the mindset of people in the West. That is why, despite the profound effect of meditation on the mind, the Western students hesitate to use meditation as a tool for discovering the inner dimensions of their lives. They see the direct correlation between mental turmoil and physical ailments, but still they prefer their disease to be cured with the help of prescriptions.

People in the West use the phrase "mind over matter," but in daily life, they practice something totally opposite. The result is that even though many teachers from the East have been teaching meditation extensively for the past thirty or forty years, meditation has not found its place among seekers. But look at the physical aspect of yoga and how popular it has become in the West! On every block you will find at least one yoga studio. In most cases, these studios do not offer classes on meditation. If they do, they are often poorly attended, considering how full their classes on yoga postures and exercise are.

Today we know so much about the body. We have gained so much knowledge of biochemistry, neurology, and pathology. Genetic engineering has become a complete field of science in itself. But all these advances have not been able to make us healthier and happier. It is my conviction that you can climb the next ladder of health and happiness only by discovering the mysteries of your mind, the hidden potential of your mind, the different faculties of your mind, and, ultimately, how your mind stands between the immortal Self and your physical self. And the wisdom of the past affirms that you can understand your mind only by making it one-pointed and inward.

The world of the mind is far bigger than the body and the world perceptible to our eyes. The world of our dreams, deep sleep, and transcendental consciousness is far bigger than the world of our waking state. The world of the waking state corresponds to this phenomenal world, which is subject to death, decay, and destruction. The world of our waking state is characterized by loss and gain, failure and success, birth and death, and therefore, is inevitably a source of fear. A person who tries to attain happiness in the waking state just by investing physical resources is bound to be met with frustration and disappointment.

If you wish to be master of yourself and your surroundings, you had best discover the part of your
mind that governs and guides the events taking place
in your waking state. You must discover how and
which part of your mind interacts with the external
world—how it colors the experiences that it gathers
from the sensory realm. You must discover which particular part of the mind functions during the dreaming state, and which particular part of the mind
remains active during deep sleep. You also have to
discover the state of consciousness that transcends
waking, dreaming, and deep sleep—the consciousness
that witnesses the activities that continuously arise
from and subside in all different parts of the mind.

Once, upon returning from the United States,
I visited my master in the Himalayas. As soon
as I approached him, he asked, "How are things in the
world?" I said, "Things in the world are fine, but
I see very few people happy." He was silent for a
while. Then, like a child, he laughed, and said,
"In their waking state, people are not happy. In their
dreaming state, people are not happy. In their
sleeping state, people are not happy. You can't make
them happy; I can't make them happy. Who is going
to make them happy?" Then he became serious and
said, "Some are seeking happiness in temples,
mosques, and churches. Others hope that they can

acquire happiness from a holy man's blessing or from a doctor's pill. People are seeking the right things but in the wrong places. That is why so far, to so many people, happiness is just a fantasy. Your job, my son, is to remind people that happiness comes from within, and that it can happen only upon knowing the mystery of one's own mind."

Everyone is in search of happiness. In fact, happiness is the most natural quest of all living beings. Some seek happiness in material achievements; others in gaining power, prestige, name, fame, and honor. In an attempt to find happiness, people exhaust all their physical and mental resources. That is how they get physically tired and mentally depleted. To help people cope with their tiredness and fatigue, nature created a system called sleep. But due to an unhealthy way of living, thinking, and being, people cannot sleep properly. Most people do not know how to turn off their minds when they no longer need to be active. Such people suffer from insomnia. In order to eliminate insomnia, they resort to medication. In the long run, medication for calming the mind and sleeping under the influence of pills causes a serious health problem. Many people stay in bed for eight to ten hours and still wake up feeling tired. What does that mean? It means the person did not sleep well. It means that during the sleeping state, the brain and nervous system continued working, thus sleep could not provide enough rest to the body.

To a certain degree, dreams are therapeutic, for they allow the mental contents stored in the unconscious mind to play out their roles. This way, the conscious mind, which has been under great pressure from the mind's unconscious contents, gets some relief. But according to the yogis, if you learn a systematic method of relaxation and calm your nervous system while remaining awake, you can become a healthier and happier person. Your need for sleep will diminish. If you meditate regularly, you will be able to cut down your dream cycle and you will not waste your time tossing and turning in bed. But in order to relax and meditate, you have to gain basic knowledge of your mind and its different faculties—how they interrelate and how they correspond to your states of waking, dreaming, and deep sleep.

The mind is an energy field. It is the finest manifestation of nature. Nature has deposited its entire bounty—all potential, capacities, and intelligence—in the mind. The mind is endowed with all creativity, both imaginable and unimaginable. The mind has the capacity to create anything it wishes. The mind has enormous space to store its unlimited experiences and keep them as long as it likes. The mind also has the capacity to store its experiences in an organized or disorganized fashion. The mind has the capacity to fool itself, too. The mind can recollect its past deeds at will, or go on living in a state of forgetfulness. The mind has the capacity to dwell on one single thought, one single idea, and one single object, or it can brood on multiple thoughts and ideas. The mind has the capacity to flow in the external world and go on running from one object to another. The mind also has the capacity to turn its face away from the external world and flow inwardly toward the center of consciousness. The mind has the capacity to function as the best friend of the body and soul or to behave like their worst enemy. Therefore, nothing in life is more important than understanding one's own mind and its relationship to oneself and the outside world.

There are two aspects of the mind—the conscious and the unconscious. It is through the conscious mind that we think, observe, analyze, reason, doubt, feel, and decide. The conscious mind remains active during our waking state. The conscious mind always works in coordination with the brain, nervous system, and sense organs. The job of the conscious mind is to gather experience from the external world. While collecting the data, it uses the senses of seeing, tasting, touching, smelling, and hearing. Upon receiving the data, the mind processes it.

Behind this whole process of collecting, analyzing, and storing data, the mind has only one purpose—to make the best use of all the gifts that life has to offer.

The conscious mind is constantly busy finding meaning and purpose in every encounter that it has with the external world. If the conscious mind is properly trained, if it is one-pointed and peaceful, it can clearly see the true meaning and purpose behind every sensory experience. But, if the mind is not disciplined, if it is confused or caught in inner turmoil, it finds no purpose and no meaning in any of its experiences. Yet driven by its instinct or habit, it goes on running after the charms and temptations of the world, only to become needlessly tired.

The purpose of meditation is to discipline the conscious mind and make it become one-pointed and tranquil. A properly trained and tranquil mind operates in a very systematic manner. On the basis of how it operates and helps us achieve the goal of life, the conscious mind is said to consist of three main faculties: *manas* (mind), *ahamkara* (ego), and *buddhi* (intellect).

Manas refers to that aspect of our conscious mind that simply receives the raw data from the external world through the senses. It is the most superficial part of the conscious mind. It doesn't involve itself in deciding whether the data is correct or incorrect, useful or not useful, beneficial or harmful. For the sake of distinguishing this part of the mind from the rest of the thinking faculty, the conscious mind, we may call manas the lower mind. It is this part of the conscious mind that conjures up limitless thoughts and ideas; it is the source of all fantasies and imaginations. And interestingly, it remains in a state of doubt regarding its own thoughts and perceptions. It lacks clarity and thus is easily swayed by sensory input.

The next faculty of the conscious mind is known as ahamkara, the part of the mind that identifies and verifies the thoughts, ideas, and feelings presented to the lower mind. Ahamkara can be loosely translated as "I-maker," or "ego." Here, the word ego has nothing to do with that that makes a person egotistical. It refers to the mental faculty that enables you to identify the objects of your thoughts and feelings in a concrete manner. It refers to the mental process that refines and takes the raw data to the next level. The ego portion of the conscious mind is like a sculptor who brings out, through his personal touch, the image that was hidden beneath the surface of the raw stone. It is the personal touch of ego that infuses sensory experiences with the feeling of "mine" and "yours," good and bad, pleasant and unpleasant. It is this faculty that colors a simple perception with the idea of good and bad and thus motivates the next and the deepest faculty, the intellect, to make a decision regarding the acquisition or elimination of the object so perceived and identified.

The intellect is the most subtle and refined aspect of the conscious mind. In the scriptures, it is described as sharp like a razor and clear like a crystal. It has the capacity to cast aside doubt and confusion. It has the capacity to clear up all false identifications. The intellect is the ruler and guide of both the lower mind and the ego. It is endowed with the capacity to see things clearly and distinguish right from wrong, good from bad, and real from unreal. Its discriminatory ability distinguishes it from two other faculties of the conscious mind—the lower mind and the ego. It has the privilege to override the advice and recommendations of the lower mind and ego.

The intellect is a repository of the power of intelligence. Its abode is next to the domain of intuition. It sees the soul, the center of consciousness, face to face. The light of pure consciousness reflects on the mirror of this aspect of the conscious mind. In the light of consciousness, the intellect is able to see clearly whether or not the thoughts, ideas, and feelings presented by the lower mind and ego are distorted. Due to its clear understanding, it can honor or reject the suggestions of the lower mind and ego. In other words, intellect is the highest authority in assessing the validity of our perception and feelings. It is the highest authority to judge whether our perceptions are correct and pure or whether they are contaminated by prejudices. As long as the intellect exercises its privilege, we perceive this world the way it is. The moment intellect becomes careless in regard to its power and privilege, it loses control over the ego and the lower mind. Then the lower mind and the ego take advantage of the intellect's carelessness. That is when they attempt to perform the intellect's job, however unsuccessfully. It is under this circumstance that we make wrong decisions. To understand what our choices are and what the criteria for making a right decision are, we must keep our intellect pure and sharp. The method that gives us access to our intellect and harnesses its intrinsic virtue—decisiveness—is called meditation.

Beyond these three faculties of the conscious mind—lower mind, ego, and intellect—lies the unconscious mind. It is the vast reservoir of all of our experiences of the past. The subtle impressions of our every thought, speech, and action are deposited in our unconscious mind. It is nature's most comprehensive database. In yogic literature, this aspect of the mind is known as *chitta*. The word *chitta* is related to the word *chit*, which means consciousness. The term *chitta* explains its own meaning—the essence of consciousness; the abstract of the functions of consciousness; the storehouse where the seeds of our past deeds are deposited. Nothing in this aspect of the mind is inert and dead, and yet we call it the unconscious mind. Why? Because people do not normally have conscious access to this part of their own mind, nor are they aware of what lies within it.

This so-called unconscious mind is like the basement of your house where years ago you stored your belongings, but for a long time, you haven't had a chance to visit. Over the years, you even forgot what you had stored there. In this long interval, your basement flooded several times, the plumbing and electrical systems became dysfunctional, and mice and other animals took over the space.

Today, you have a hard time entering this dark and musty basement. You have neither the convenience nor the capacity to take an inventory of your long-deposited belongings. For all practical purposes, you have abandoned your basement, but it is still *your* basement. Long-forgotten belongings sitting in your basement are *your* belongings. When you move to your next house, it is your responsibility to dispose of those belongings or to take them with you. In either case, you have to enter your basement. You cannot escape your past. You cannot escape the fruits of your past deeds. You must face them. You must do something with them. Your lack of awareness regarding the contents in the basement of your mind does not make those contents vanish. In your ignorance, you may go on proclaiming that they don't exist, but sooner or later, reality hits. Then you realize that the vast storehouse of your past, in its own right, is fully conscious, very actively alive. Those impressions exert their influence on you, regardless of whether you are awake or asleep, conscious or unconscious.

For a vigilant and awakened person, there is nothing like the unconscious mind. Similarly, for a careless and unawakened person, there is no conscious mind. A person familiar with the dynamics of the so-called unconscious mind performs his actions with full awareness and attains freedom from the bondage of karma. A person not familiar with these dynamics performs his actions without knowing what is compelling him to undertake them, further entangling himself in the bondage of karma. Therefore, creating a bridge between the conscious and unconscious mind and illuminating both with each other's light is crucial to attaining peace and happiness here and now. Meditation is the way to create the bridge between these two aspects of the mind.

The unconscious mind has an enormous influence over the conscious mind. Quite often, we know what is right, and yet we do not feel motivated to do it. We also know what is wrong, but we do not know how to stop doing it. This happens because the contents in the unconscious mind keep influencing our conscious mind—its thoughts, feelings, and behaviors. It is only when we begin to meditate that we realize how vast our unconscious mind is and how potent are its contents. In fact, our personality is determined by what we are internally. Our inner make-up consists of our unconscious contents. We may not know what those contents are, and yet we think, feel, and express ourselves in accordance with our inner make-up. For this reason, some of us are naturally loving, kind, and giving, while others are aggressive and unforgiving. Therefore, to understand the mystery of life and bring a lasting transformation within and without, we have to dive deep into the depths of our own unconscious minds.

To further describe the nature of the unconscious mind, let me tell you an ancient story. A long time ago, there lived a great yogi. He was one of the most disciplined meditators of his time. He mastered asana, the yogic postures, and thus cultivated an unimaginable degree of endurance and fortitude. He could sit for several days in meditation without any movement. He could concentrate his mind on an object without the slightest fluctuation.

One day, he withdrew his mind from the realm of the senses and focused it at the eyebrow center. Soon he reached such a high level of concentration that he was no longer aware of the external world. His lower mind, ego, and intellect stood still. Finally, he crossed the realm of the conscious mind and entered the vast storehouse of his past impressions. There, through his inwardly turned consciousness, he saw the endless accumulations of his past. He saw himself as a loving father; but then, in another life, he found himself as a snake, devouring the same children whom he loved so much in his other life. He was confronted with memories filled with utter extremes and contrasts. It was as though someone turned on an enormous light, enabling him to see everything that lay in the basement of his mind all at once.

The yogi was both thrilled and puzzled. He was happy that he had gained access to the vast reservoir of his memory; but at the same time, he was saddened, for he realized how much cleanup he had to do before he could free himself from the fruits of all his past deeds. This realization unearthed a long chain of questions and queries—when did the journey of life begin? When and why did I perform my first action? When did the chain of karma begin? How did I come under the influence of desire and attachment in the first place? What is the way of removing my karmic stains? Is it ever possible to be free from karmic influence? Is it ever possible to attain complete freedom from ego, attachment, desire, and fear? Is it possible to throw away one's unconscious contents? Are our thoughts, speech, and actions always governed by our unconscious mind? Can the conscious mind, especially the intellect, make its decision independently? Are we totally a product of the past, and does our future depend on a present that is a slave to the past? Who created this unconscious mind, and why? Seeking answers to these questions, the yogi visited an adept named Avatya.

Avatya is one of the greatest masters of all times. He is regarded as Yogishwara—the Lord of Yogis. Upon hearing the questions put forth by this great yogi, Avatya answered, "How much or how little you know about your unconscious mind and its contents is immaterial. What really matters is the realization that it is vast and its contents are numberless. Its depth is unfathomable. Upon realizing its vastness, simply create a powerful bridge between your conscious and unconscious mind. Fill your unconscious with the light of your *buddhi*, which is infused with the power of right understanding and decisiveness. Use your right understanding to practice dispassion and non-attachment in relation to your past, should it become known to your conscious mind, just as you do in relation to your present. This meditative approach to dealing with your unconscious mind and its content will help you calm down inner unrest, and thereafter all other aspects of your mind will be free from all troubles, sorrows, fears, and worries caused by that inner unrest."

The power of the unconscious mind is immense. Although its contents were at some point created or at least gathered by the three faculties of the conscious mind, once there, they exert an enormous influence on those three faculties—lower mind, ego, and intellect. If you pay attention, you will notice that your perception of this world and of the people around you is often quite distorted. That is because your lower mind is under the influence of your unconscious contents; your distorted view of others is further passed on to your ego. If your ego lacks purity and inner strength, then it will take its action on the basis of that distorted view. In this situation, the ego's performance will result in false identification. Your understanding of that person or the object will not be accurate. Your mistaken understanding of that person is then passed on to your intellect. If your intellect is not pure and sharp, it will take that mistaken understanding for real. Its judgment will be based on false understanding.

With this kind of mind, you are bound to make mistakes. The important thing, therefore, is to free your mind of distorted perception, false identification, and misjudgment. You can do this only if you know something about your unconscious mind and its latent contents. You must also know how the subtle impressions stored in your unconscious mind may become awakened, and thereafter, how they govern your conscious faculty. The process that allows you to peek into your unconscious mind is called self-study—the study of yourself by yourself. Self-study is possible only when you have acquired a basic level of concentration in your lower mind, the purification of your ego, and the sharpening of your intellect.

You are a human being. You must not say that this kind of self-study, which leads to your self-understanding and the understanding of mind, ego, and intellect, is beyond your capacity. Many in the past have done it, and you can, too. This is where you must cultivate trust in your self-effort; and when you put your whole heart in this endeavor, divine grace will definitely come to your aid. You must always remind yourself, "God created humans in His own image." You are, in every respect, not just a reflection of God, but a replica of God. The unmanifest has become manifest in the form of you. If God means Creator, then the Creator's creativity is in you. If God means beauty, then that beauty is you, and is in you. If God means love, then that love is you. If God means the power to be and the power to become, then that power is you, and therefore, you have the capacity to become whatever you wish.

A human being who doesn't have faith in his intimate relationship with God suffers from inner poverty. He is like a boat lost in the ocean. Self-trust is the ground for cultivating this faith. That is why the scriptures say, "Ye, why seek thyself, thy master, outside thee?" Once you understand something about your eternity and oneness with the Supreme, your conscious mind becomes charged with the power of will and determination, and thereafter, the undesirable contents of your unconscious mind have no power to influence your thoughts, speech, and actions.

The seeds of your destiny lie in your unconscious mind. If you have not learned the art of managing your unconscious mind, then you are a victim of your destiny. If you do not pay attention to your habit patterns and their impact on your thoughts, speech, and actions, then you are nothing more than destiny's football. It is your carelessness and your lack of trust in yourself that allows you to be tossed and kicked around by destiny. Did you ever pause for a moment and realize that you are the creator of your own destiny? God has no interest in making you miserable, nor does God have interest in making Himself miserable by constantly worrying about you. God invested all of His powers in you and said, "From now on, you, the finest of my creation, be the creator of your destiny." Thus was born the human race.

Let me explain how you are the creator of your destiny and how you go on collecting the building blocks of your present and your future. You are blessed with the power of will and determination. Linear thinking is your unique virtue. You can think, examine, verify, and decide. You can translate your

thoughts into speech and actions. Due to your retentive power, you can clearly see the concomitant relationship between cause and effect. You can clearly see
what you did in the past and what the results were.
Based on that, you have the capacity to decide what
you should or should not do in the present. This way,
you can predict the outcome of your present action.

Yogis call this process the anatomy of karma. In
simpler language, the dynamics of this anatomy is
described by the phrase "as you sow, so shall you
reap." The subtle impressions of every single action
you perform go into your memory. As you repeat
the same or similar actions, the impressions keep getting stronger and heavier. There comes a time when
the subtle impressions of your previous deeds become
so powerful that they begin to influence your conscious mind. Under the influence of those impressions, the mind motivates you to perform new sets of
similar actions. Once this wheel of action is set in
motion, you have a hard time stopping it. This is
called the unconscious over the conscious mind—
habits motivating your thoughts, speech, and actions.
If you do not pay attention, all three faculties of the
mind will then become victim of their own past
actions. A vigilant person, however, has the capacity to
look back, summon his willpower and determination,
and declare, "I am going to break this cycle. I am

going to render the subtle impressions of my past dead. I am going to create a new mindset, new thoughts, new ideas, and I am going to perform such actions that will counteract the impressions of my unwanted deeds. I am going to set the wheel of new patterns in motion. I am going to pull out only such seeds of my past that promise a desirable harvest." This is called mustering the power of will and deter-mination, *sankalpa shakti*, the divine quality that has allowed humans to exceed all other living beings on the planet.

Brooding on the past and worrying about the future is a sure sign and symptom that you have not made any attempt to discover your own hidden wealth. When I hear people consulting astrology, I feel pity for them. Don't you see that you are nearer to yourself than any planet, star, or constellation in the universe? Is there any star bigger than your mind? Is there any light that runs faster than your mind? Is there any celestial body that shines brighter than your mind? Is there any friend who can render his help in a more lasting fashion than your mind? Is anyone more reliable than your own mind? Then why do you not learn the art of embracing your mind? Why do you not learn the art of making it more friendly than it is now? Here I recast the message of ancient masters, the enlightened ones, who saw the truth face to face, "Safeguard your mind, for once it is safe, the whole world will be safe." Leave the external crutches such as astrology, temples, mosques, churches, pandits, priests, and swamis behind, and march on the path of self-discovery and self-mastery, which begins with the discovery of and the mastery over your own mind.

— Chapter Four —

Happiness Is Your Creation

AS I MENTIONED EARLIER, I BECAME AN ORPHAN AT an early age and grew up with my master, a saint who lived away from the crowd. His dwellings were simple: either a cave or a thatched hut. His food usually consisted of two dishes—vegetables and bread, or rice and dahl, for example. A simple mattress on the ground served as his bed. Most of the time, he sat with his eyes closed. Throughout the day and night, he spoke only a few sentences. In his company, I felt like I was prince of the universe, but I did not know why. When I entered my adolescence, my master remarked, "This world and worldly objects can provide some degree of comfort, but they have no power to make you happy. God created you, but it is you who must create your happiness." I pondered his comments and I thought I understood what he meant—but in truth, I didn't.

Then I joined Woodstock, one of India's most prestigious high schools, located in the foothills of the Himalayas. My master provided all the material means that I needed to live there just as the children of British officers and the children of wealthy Indians lived. Many of the royalty of India were my master's disciples and followers. Whenever they visited, they brought money and offered it at his feet. Sadhus had no use for money, so I was the only one to spend it.

As long as I was in the mountains, money had no value. Nothing beyond the bare necessities was available even if you had a lot of money. But at Woodstock I learned how to live lavishly. There, I bought several Gramophones and a large number of records. One summer, with all of these fancy belongings, I went to see my master. Previously, I used to visit him by myself; this time, I needed porters. Upon seeing me, he said, "It makes me happy to see you growing. What are these porters carrying?"

When I told him that they were Gramophones, he giggled like a child and said, "Let me hear how they sound!" I turned one of them on. At this, he said, "What about the others? Turn all of them on!"

I told him that you can't hear all of them at once, but he insisted. I could not understand why he was demanding that I play all the Gramophones together.

I knew that arguing with him was futile, so I put different records on each Gramophone and played them together. With a sense of disapproval, he made a face and said, "What is this gibberish? I don't understand this noise."

I argued, "That's why I was telling you that you play only one record at a time."

At this, he responded, "If you cannot enjoy more than one piece of music at a time, then why do you need more than one Gramophone?" Still, I did not get the point. For the next several days, he made many remarks, most of them without context: "I want to see you happy. . . . I want you to grow up and become a healthy man. . . . Learn to cultivate a lifestyle that is both tasteful and purposeful. . . . Do not let your happiness be dependent on worldly failures and achievements. . . . "

That summer, he also spoke about the importance of spiritual wisdom and esoteric experiences. He told me of the power of mantras and how the proper practice of mantra can make you become successful in the world. He convinced me that the miraculous powers that many yogis possess come from mantra practice. Anyone who has become rich and influential had done lots of mantra repetition, he said, either in this lifetime or in a previous one. Very soon, I was convinced that if I received one of those master mantras, I would succeed in my studies; I would become rich and famous, a celebrity both in the spiritual and mundane realms. My desire to find a master who could teach me the most powerful mantra was kindled. When my master knew that I was fully ready to undertake any spiritual discipline to become a successful person, he told me about one such master who lived in Rishikesh. Without wasting any time, I went to visit this great saint.

As soon as I reached this master, he asked me the purpose of my visit. When I told him, he said, "I don't have time to teach you."

I asked him, "How long do I have to stay before you can teach me?"

He said, "A month. Perhaps two, or even more."

Knowing the gravity of the knowledge that I wished to receive from him, I made up my mind to stay as long as he wanted. For a couple of weeks, he didn't pay attention to me. Then he became more considerate. One day he told me that he knew my master very well, and he also knew how much my master loved me; therefore, he would give the knowledge that he normally shared only with the most prepared students. He told me that tomorrow was going to be a very auspicious day, and that I should take a bath, put on clean clothes, and meet him at the bank of the Ganga in the morning.

I was so excited, I couldn't sleep the whole night. In the morning, I met him at the bank of the Ganga. He

instructed me to sit in my meditation posture facing
him. He remained silent for several minutes. Then he
said, "In all situations and circumstances in life, try to
be happy. This is the highest mantra that I can give to
you today. Even if you are behind bars, be happy. You
may be the creation of your destiny, but happiness is
your creation. Happiness is the most personal virtue
of your soul. No one can give you happiness and no
one can take your happiness away from you. If you
have not learned the art of happiness, then no matter
what else you have achieved in life, you are no more
than a beggar."

Happiness is a subject that concerns everyone. It
concerned the ancient ones, and it is our concern
today. Throughout history, we have been trying to
understand how we can be happy. We always think
that people somewhere else are happier than we are.
But that is not true. All over the world, I see people
suffering from a great deal of restlessness; people are
trying to reach that place that can make them happy;
they are trying to obtain the objects they assume
will make them happy. Upon deep reflection and
observation, I see the reason why human beings have
not yet achieved happiness—it is because they have
not yet been able to understand the exact source of
happiness. No matter where you live, no matter what
you have in the external world, and no matter how
many things you own, if you have not understood the

source of happiness, and if you cannot reach it, you cannot be happy at all.

Human beings have a big problem—they prefer to see things only in black and white. They divide the whole world into two categories: good and bad. They put all actions in two categories: right and wrong. This tendency leads them to become judgmental, and their labeling becomes the ground for conflict, dispute, and war. What people do not realize is that things in the world are not black and white. There are numberless grades in their shapes, sizes, colors, and tastes. So is the case with right and wrong, good and bad. As soon as you rise above the narrow confines of your preconceived notions, prejudices, and preoccupations, you will begin to see that neither the objects of the world nor people are good or bad; rather it is your understanding of them that makes them good or bad. Let me give you a living example that is common in all cultures of the world.

Every culture has its mythology. Mythology is made of two sets of entities: gods and demons. There is always a war between these gods and demons. They hate each other. In order to vanquish each other, they apply all possible tactics, from wits to tricks. The gods are as busy hunting down demons as the demons are hunting down gods. While at war, both groups are equally miserable. Both of them suffer from fear and anxiety. In the search for peace and happiness, both

groups resort to austerity, seeking boons from someone higher than themselves.

In Indian mythology, both celestial and demonic
beings are children of a great sage, Kashyapa, and two
of his wives. Both sets of children grew up in the same
household and received the same kind of love and
education. Yet from the very beginning, they thought
of themselves as totally separate from each other.
Both of them tried to excel by demeaning each other.
By the time they were adults, they were very well
steeped in their unique ways of thinking and being.
They developed respect for values that were different
from each other. Up to this point, there wasn't much
conflict in their household. However, there came a
time when both groups became adamant about their
values and ideas. They began to impose their philosophy and worldviews on each other. When one group
refused, the other felt insulted. The more they
imposed on each other, the more animosity grew.
Both parties labeled each other as villains; one did not
tolerate the existence of the other. This attitude led
them to repeated wars.

The scriptures document a repeated cycle of war
between these two groups, describing how brutally
they fought and how much bloodshed they caused.
Both groups were God-minded people, but in their
own ways. Brothers from both parties committed
themselves to intense spiritual practices and austerities,

but only with the intention of gaining power to domi-
nate and condemn each other. Both parties remained a
source of misery to themselves and to the whole world,
until one day, the Manushya (children of another sage
named Manu) discovered how to be happy without
making anyone miserable. Through their deep contemplation, self-reflection, and inwardly turned minds,
the children of Manu realized that happiness can grow
only from the domain of pure love.

Love means to give, to share, and to serve selflessly.
Love is alive when it is sustained by selflessness and
contentment. Expectation is a deadly disease that kills
love. And a person without love becomes hollow and
suffers from emptiness. The children of Manu, who
gained and prized this understanding, exceeded both
the gods and the demons, for they attained freedom
from all conflicts within and without. Do you know
who these children of Manu are? Human beings. The
word for humans in the Sanskrit language is
Manushya, which literally means Manu's offspring.
Therefore, it is the infusion of love that makes one
become truly human.

In the Indian tradition, Manu, the father of the
human race, holds a more important place than all the
prophets, saviors, and messiahs combined. Just by
knowing who this Manu is, what he did, and what he
passed on to his children, you, too, will be proud of
being a descendant of this great soul. Manu is the son

of the Sun. He is said to be as radiant as his father, for in Manu resides the light of the Sun. Long ago, he lived a peaceful and tranquil life and had several children. He taught them the art of joyful living. Long ago, Manu taught them, "That which is rightfully yours cannot be taken away from you. But do not try to lay your hands on that which is not yours, for you cannot succeed in claiming it. Be happy with what you have; aspire to obtain what you need, and use everything to attain the highest purpose of life."

Manu taught his children to work hard without worrying about the fruits of their actions. His fame as a wise man spread far and wide. Learned people from all over the land came to learn the art of happiness from him. Then there arrived the most crucial moment in the history of creation. One day, as part of his daily worship, Manu was offering water to the god Sun. Suddenly, he noticed a tiny fish in the water, which he picked up and held in his palm. The fish told him about a great flood that would envelop the face of the earth and advised him, "Gather the seed of everything that exists in creation and deposit those seeds in a boat. Along with the Seven Sages, board the boat. I will return to you again and pull the boat to safety."

The great flood came as predicted. The seeds of every aspect of creation were already on the boat. Accompanied by the Seven Sages, Manu rode the boat. The fish returned with the grandeur compatible to the size of the seven seas combined and pulled the boat to the higher peaks of the Himalayas where Manu, the custodian of all that existed before, made his dwelling. In the Sanskrit language, the word *Manu* refers to the essence of mind. The power that lies at the core of the mind, the power that breathes life into the mind, the light that illuminates the mind is called Manu. Nature has invested its bounty in the mind. When the mind is calm and tranquil, it is able to see both ends of the present—past and future.

That is why the tranquil Manu, the mind, could foresee the calamity that was on its way. As a custodian of the future, he did not judge which particular seed was right or wrong, good or bad. He preserved them all, for he knew that diversity is essential to prosperity. He loved both the bright and dark aspects of creation, and that is why he was given the privilege to stock everything on his ark and safeguard it until the seeds found their rightful place in Nature's courtyard. Human beings are blessed children of this great sage, the peaceful and enlightened mind. I hope and I pray that the human race, the children of this great soul, discover their unique privilege—to love all and hate none—the privilege they have received as an inheritance from Manu, the privilege that makes them fully mature humans.

Before coming to the West, my world was confined

to a handful of sadhus who lived in solitude and villagers who were content with whatever little they had. Theirs was a life of simplicity. Giving and sharing were a part of life. Peace and contentment followed them as their shadows. When I visited cities and stayed with wealthy people, I was struck with a bewildering reality—the more people had, the unhappier they were. I could not understand it. When I came to the West, this reality presented itself in a much more vivid manner. Here, people had everything they needed to live a comfortable life, and yet I found husbands and wives fighting with each other. I saw a society full of broken families. I tried to understand why people rush into divorce. What do they achieve by getting rid of each other? How can parents ever be happy when they see their children suffering on account of their divorce? What are they seeking outside their marriage? What do they gain by getting married again to someone else?

I talked with a large number of psychologists, counselors, and therapists. All of them shared with me one common experience: "Swamiji, fear has reached the deepest recess of the psyche of this culture. People are afraid of themselves; they are afraid of each other. Fear has robbed them of their trust in themselves and in others. In an attempt to cope with this fear, they try to create a wall of self-protection that is as thick and high as possible. In today's world, this wall of self-protection is called security. People are so concerned with security, you cannot even imagine." These were educated and experienced professionals. I knew them personally, and I had no reason to discredit their experience.

At the eve of my life, I urge you to listen and to embrace the message of the great enlightened souls: "Why do you suffer from fear and insecurity, oh children of immortality! Lack of trust in yourselves and in your loved ones is clear evidence that you have not known yourselves. Love is your origin. Your journey of life begins from the pool of love. Deep within, you are carrying this inexhaustible wealth of love. It continues growing as you spend it. With the magic touch of your love, you can awaken others to discover the same. Upon discovering their own source, the inexhaustible love, they will no longer fear you; they will no longer curl up and shrink inside the dead shells of their insecurity and mistrust. They will gladly open their hearts to you. The opening of these hearts will welcome Spring, both in your life as well as in theirs."

I know many people who do not want to hurt themselves and definitely do not want to harm anyone else. And yet, due to their rigidity in relation to their views, they go on labeling themselves and others. Some of them suffer from self-righteousness and others from self-condemnation. All of them wish to be happy and to share their happiness with others. But they don't succeed in achieving their wishes because they do not know how to overcome their rigid mindset.

Here, I will narrate an incident that took place at the Himalayan Institute. At the Institute we have a program called the Self-Transformation Program. It is a residential, month-long program designed to offer an opportunity for participants to identify their strengths and weaknesses, discover their short-term and long-term goals, bring regularity into their lives, overcome habits that create obstacles in their journey, and, finally, get established in their personal practice. The program coordinators and instructors ran the entire program. Participants made appointments with me only when they sought personal counseling or mantra initiation. Occasionally, participants came to me with complaints. On one such occasion, a student offered me advice about how to improve the quality of the program. He said, "Swami Rama, the Institute should have a private lounge for happy people. It bothers me to be around unhappy people. In fact, I don't understand why you allow them to come to the Institute, for their presence pollutes the peaceful atmosphere here. You have beautiful grounds, good food, and a good program, but these unhappy people are like dead fish in a pond."

I said to the gentleman, "You should feel good that an unhappy person has come into the company of a happy person like you. It should not bother you; it should not make you upset. Are you upset?"

"Of course, Swami Rama," he responded. "In fact, now I am more upset. I thought you would be open to constructive criticism, but you don't seem to understand. I am a happy man. Why should I allow unhappy people to be around me? What kind of transformation will I experience if I let my cheerful energy be sucked out of me by these people?"

I asked, "How did you manage your life before coming here? How many people around you did not disturb your happiness?"

He exclaimed, "That's why I came here! Nobody understands me. I am a happy person. I am a good person. I don't harm anybody. I deserve to be left alone. No one has a right to disturb me. All I am asking for is my right."

I counseled him, "My friend, I will tell the accounting office to give you back twice the fee you paid for the Self-Transformation Program. Leave this Institute, which fails to exclude unhappy people. But please, do me a favor. Wherever and whenever you find a place inhabited only by happy people, please let me know. I will join that community. And if you ever find a technique for creating such a community, please share it with me. I promise I will dedicate my whole life to promoting that technique." These, and other opinionated views that rob our peace and happiness, have their roots in one single fact—lack of self-understanding.

Now, let me tell you clearly that you will be the happiest person on the planet when you know who you are, where you have come from, what your purpose is in being here, and where you will go when you leave this world. Therefore, through your thoughts, speech, and actions, try to understand the meaning and purpose of life. You have all the tools and means to succeed in this endeavor. Human beings are the most blessed species; not only are they on the top of the food chain, but also they are fully equipped to make the best use of all the resources this world has to offer. There is nothing that a human being cannot accomplish. Therefore, it is totally your choice whether you want to be happy or simply live at the mercy of destiny. Finding meaning and purpose in life is as simple as eating, sleeping, and breathing, provided you mobilize all the resources you have within and without.

From your childhood you have been told that the purpose of life is to find God. You do not know what God is, and yet you spend your time talking about God and looking for God. Be realistic. Pay attention and try to understand, at this particular stage in your life, what you must do and must not do, what your real duties are and what your secondary duties are. When you look at yourself with a calm and tranquil mind, you will find that you have biological urges, certain duties and obligations toward yourself and to those who are near and dear to you. There are some karmic connections between you and your loved ones. You have no choice but to fulfill your duties toward those you claim to love. Do not try to run away from your duties, for the call of duty will bring you back to this world. Just because your temple, priest, or guru has been saying that God is the goal of life, you cannot ignore your duties. If you do not pay attention to who you are and what your relationship with this world is, you are bound to be confused.

I have faith in God, for I know God is the Lord of Life. Leave me with my conviction. For your good, however, I tell you that God is not your top priority. Your top priority is to know yourself at every level. Assess your present level of physical capacity, emotional maturity, and intellectual grasp. Assess the level of your inner strength and willpower. Assess all the resources lined up in your immediate environment and put together a plan to use everything you have to achieve your highest goal. This is called being practical. No one can define you; no one can decide your goals and your purpose in life. If you decide for yourself, and if your decision is based on an honest assessment of your strengths and weaknesses, you will have fewer distractions and disturbances. You will not have to waste your time and energy fighting with obstacles. You will devote the greater part of your time and energy to becoming successful, both here and hereafter. Then you will know where God fits in your personal life, and you'll be happy to know where you fit in the grand scheme of God.

There is no use knowing God without knowing who you are. History is filled with people who claimed that they knew God, but after such proclamations, their misery did not seem to vanish. Seeing God and attaining self-realization are two different things. Seeing God automatically includes knowing yourself, as well as your relationship with the higher truth. This self-realization makes you fearless. It instills your mind and heart with indomitable will and trust in Providence. Regarding God and self-realization, I will share with you one of my experiences with my master.

Living with my master afforded me the opportunity to sit for several hours in meditation in early childhood. Meanwhile, my knowledge of the scriptures kindled my desire to see God. The scriptures also made me believe that the more I meditated, the closer meditation would take me to seeing God. At the age of seventeen, I became very frustrated because after so many hours of daily meditation, I still had not seen God. One day, I told my master that he was not a genuine teacher, that he lacked compassion and concern for his students. I complained that when wandering sadhus came to him, he spent time with them and then they went away happily, clearly showing that they received something very profound and meaningful from him. At the climax of my complaint, I said, "I have been living in your company since my childhood and still I am a fool. You had better show me God, or tomorrow morning I will leave you."

With a smile, he said, "I am happy that now you are ready. Tomorrow morning, I will definitely show you God."

Because I was so excited, I could not sleep the whole night. Before sunrise, I took a bath in the Ganga, put on my cleanest clothes, and prostrated myself before my master. Anxiety made me nervous. I was trying to be as humble as possible, for I had heard it is humility that prepares one to receive the highest wisdom. I was hoping that my master would recite some mantra to invoke God. But instead, he said, "What kind of God do you want to see, my son?"

I had never considered this question. I exclaimed, "Are there types of Gods?"

He said, "Of course. You must have some concept of God. If I show you a God that is not compatible with your understanding, how are you going to believe that it is God? First tell me the image of God that you hold in your mind." When I told him that I did not know how to conceive the idea of God, he said, "You have no idea what kind of God you want to see, and yet you want to see Him."

This encounter with my master made me both sad and happy at once. I realized that my desire to know God had no substance. It lacked content. I was running after a concept of God just because I had been hearing that there is a God and that the vision of God takes away all pains and miseries. Until this time, I had never paid attention to whether I was really interested in seeing God or in finding happiness here and now.

I was surprised to know that I was seeking something without knowing what it was. When I told my master about my confusion, he said, "In this world of confusion and disorientation, my son, you are not alone. Millions of people are working hard seeking something without knowing what it is. And that is why they reach nowhere. It is after knowing who you are that you will understand what you want to become. This knowledge will infuse your mind and heart with clarity; it will drive away all doubts and fears. It will make you self-confident. It will help you set priorities in life; then you will know exactly where and how God-realization fits into your life. You can build a beautiful structure of God-realization only on the firm foundation of self-realization."

Self-realization consists of knowing two aspects of

yourself—lower and higher selves. The lower self is made of your body, breath, mind, ego, and intellect. Most often, our consciousness is confined to this level of self. We exhaust a greater part of our time and energy in attending the needs and demands of this lower self. Our loss and gain, honor and insult, and success and failure are associated with the lower self. This part of us is subject to birth and death. The experience of pleasure and pain is integral to this part of ourselves. The mind is the leader of this lower self. Using the senses as a tool, the mind attaches itself to the external world. The mind knows only how to see the world outside itself. It runs from one object to another. It goes on labeling some objects as pleasant and others as unpleasant. The mind's tendency is to cling to the pleasant and despise the unpleasant. Upon losing the pleasant, it suffers. When met by the unpleasant, it suffers. Thus the mind's inability to find inner repose keeps it in perpetual misery.

Due to its strong association with the mind, the lower self is in the habit of identifying itself with everything that it holds dear. It is this tendency that makes us identify ourselves as Christian or Hindu, Eastern or Western, rich or poor. Every object in the world with which we identify is constantly changing, but lacking true knowledge, we don't comprehend the eternal law of change. Thus, while seeing, we do not see. While experiencing, we do not experience. We remain blind to the reality that is so simple and clear.

The higher self lies at the core of our being. It is eternal. Pure consciousness is its intrinsic nature. Purity of knowledge defines its character. Confusion cannot reach it. It is the light of this higher self that illuminates the lower self. It is the perennial source of healing and nourishment. At this level, we experience our oneness with the universal consciousness. In the scriptures written in the Sanskrit language, this higher self is called *Atman*, which can be translated as "soul." When Jesus Christ says, "I and my father are one in the same," he is referring to this level of the self. It is upon knowing the higher self that the pleasure and pain, good and bad, and the concepts of virtue and sin lose their impact. Self-realization means to know both levels of reality—the lower and higher—and gain a clear understanding of how these two levels relate to each other. When our lower self begins to operate in the light of the higher one, we experience a spiritual freedom, a release from the troubles caused by the unwholesome understanding and activity of the lower self. From the womb of this spiritual freedom manifests the perennial joy that all of us are seeking. We attain this spiritual freedom when we gain access to the core of our being, the higher self. To reach there, we must organize all of the faculties that are part of our lower self. The process that enables us to organize all of those faculties and gain access to the core of our being is called meditation. We may learn a great deal about the anatomy of pleasure and pain, happiness and sorrow, but it is meditation that can transform our understanding into an experiential one. Thus, meditation is the way to claim the joy that lies within.

Chapter Five

Happy Forever

HAPPINESS IS A VIRTUE OF A POSITIVE MIND, WHILE pain is the fruit of a negative mind. By cultivating a positive mind, you can be happy; and by holding on to a negative mind, you can be miserable. Cultivating a positive mind requires that you first cultivate a right understanding of yourself and others. You fill your worldview with a proper attitude. You build a philosophy of life that is founded on a positive attitude. You simplify your life and minimize your expectations of others. Be realistic and stop living in the world of fantasy. You will become happy, and you will remain happy forever. To clarify my point, let me share my experience with you.

I was living in England. One day, a gentleman visited me with his girlfriend. He introduced her to me and said, "Swamiji, this is my girlfriend. I want to marry her. Please give me your blessings."

I wasn't very inspired to bless this couple. I felt that there was something wrong between the two, and especially with the young man. So I asked him, "Why do you want to marry her?"

With bewilderment, the young man responded, "Because I love her, Swamiji."

I was not satisfied with his answer, so I asked, "Why do you love her?"

"Because she is beautiful," he answered.

Spontaneously, I said, "That's not enough. You have to have a better reason than that to marry her. However, when you do get married, please come; I will give my blessings to both of you."

One morning, before going to the office, the young man stopped at his girlfriend's apartment. It was early, and she was still in bed. He rang the bell. She jumped out of bed and opened the door. The young man, holding a rose in his hand, exclaimed, "Surprise!"

But in the next moment, upon seeing her face and disheveled hair, he was shocked. All he could say was, "I can't believe it!" and left. All day long, he remained disturbed. In the evening, he came to me and said, "Swamiji, it is shocking! She is not beautiful at all! In fact, she is ugly. Thank you for not giving your blessings, otherwise I could have rushed into marrying her."

When I asked him how he found out that she wasn't beautiful, he told me the whole story. I counseled him, "My son, to find beauty, you must go beyond the skin. Beauty contained in a cosmetic bottle is very superficial. It doesn't last, and definitely it cannot become the ground for true love. To see real beauty, you must train your mind to peer into your own heart, as well as into the heart of others."

In any relationship, it is not physical beauty that attracts you. If that were the case, then all high school boys would have been attracted to just a few girls. There are men and women with different features, and almost all of them, sooner or later, become attracted to someone. That means that beauty lies in the eye of the beholder. The initial thrust that brings two individuals closer to each other is more than physical beauty. That may be a trigger, but it is the beauty of the heart, and the beauty of thoughts, feelings, and ideas that sustains the attraction and gradually transforms it into a deeper form of love. Love is sustained by selflessness. When both parties derive joy from giving the best of themselves to each other, then it means they are operating on the ground of pure love. Joy, springing from this love, is everlasting. This form of love is immortal, for it remains alive even after your loved one is gone.

The power and wisdom that stems from pure love is the foundation for building a healthy family and society. A family's riches are not measured by how much wealth they have accumulated, but rather, by how much love the family members have for each other; how much happiness they experience by serving and caring for each other selflessly; how much concern they have for each other's health and happiness; and how spontaneously they come forward to share each other's sorrow. Being born in such a family is the greatest fortune. Creating such a family atmosphere is the most glorious act; maintaining such an atmosphere is the greatest responsibility; and passing on that atmosphere to the next generation is the highest form of service.

Now I will share with you another experience that will give you an idea about how we contaminate our love, and in the process, ruin our happiness. A famous astronaut visited me frequently. Once in a while, he brought his wife with him. At face value, they appeared to be very happy people, but I felt there was a great deal of resentment between them. I could not understand why. The husband was famous; the wife was beautiful. What else did they need to be proud of and happy with each other? One day, during a private appointment, I asked her, "What is bothering you?" With her eyes filled with tears, she said, "Swamiji, once famous, my husband became arrogant. He no longer behaves like my husband; he expects me to adore him because he is an astronaut. If I don't behave like his fan, he gets mad at me. We are not happy with each other. I need your help to keep my family together."

When you identify yourself with your success or failure, you are bound to isolate yourself from your loved ones. Respect for what you are is totally different from being arrogant about who you are. Self-respect infuses your mind and heart with honor and dignity, transforming you into an honorable and dignified person. Then you will automatically be pulled into the nucleus of your family and the larger world around you, and people will naturally be attracted by your magnetism. They will gravitate toward you. You will become the recipient of people's spontaneous love. You will not fear anyone, and no one will fear you. The atmosphere of fearlessness within and without is the ground for lasting peace and happiness.

Let me give you another example of how a strong identification with your spiritual image can take away the purity of your love, causing a lack of harmony in your family and society. I know a very learned person. He is an expert in several languages. He is a prolific writer and speaker. He is the founder of several religious organizations. Since early adulthood, he has been hailed as a guru, a spiritual teacher. The woman he married was at one point his student. Before marriage, she adored him for his wisdom. He, too, welcomed her, for he sensed how well she understood him. This spiritual recognition from both sides became ground for the intimacy that matured into marriage. After marriage, however, the reality changed.

They started their life together as a married couple. A large number of students who had been impressed with the guru for his abstinence and his lack of involvement in worldly matters changed their opinions of him and left. The pain caused by injury to his spiritual image intensified when his wife also expected him to behave like a husband. Soon, they were parents of two children. That is when they met me. When they sought my help, I advised them, "It is man and woman who have turned into husband and wife. Therefore, be normal and act normally. You will be happy." Then I turned to the man and said, "Your strong identification with your spiritual image is causing distress to your family. The more you impose your spiritual stature, the more your wife will resent you. The more you demand respect, the less of it you will have. While living in a family, you are happy when you are loving, kind, and open to sharing each other's thoughts and feelings. People are comfortable with you when you do not mask your personality. Do not try to convince the members of your family about who you are, for they know you very well. Be spontaneous. Do not force the members of your family to learn from you. If there is anything worth learning, they will learn it automatically. But remember, whatever lies within you emits its energy in the outside world. If the energy within you, regardless of how spiritual it is, is emitted with the intention of dominating others, it will cause unrest."

Evidently, this highly educated man did not hear me. He has been teaching throughout the country and visits me regularly. His family, too, respects me very much, but I find myself helpless upon seeing them, especially the teenage children who have become totally rebellious against the values that had been imposed on them.

Life means relationship. How you manage your relationships is indicative of how you are managing your life. Every relationship has its own beauty, charm, and place in life. In relation to your wife, play your husbandly role. In relation to your children, play your parental role. In relation to your students, you are a teacher, and in relation to your teacher, you are a student. While playing these roles, make sure that you are free from all conflicts; make sure that you are clear and sincere. Perform your duties skillfully, lovingly, and selflessly. You can do that when you do not identify yourself with your action, with your role, and with the outcome of the relationship. That is what will make you free from fear and anxiety, and you will begin to be here and now.

A relationship that is contaminated by an inferiority/superiority complex is a source of misery. Regardless of how spiritual your complex is, it is, after all, a complex.

It is all right to be attracted to someone's spiritual wisdom, but using spirituality to form a worldly relationship is shear ignorance. A relationship grounded in ignorance leads you to disappointment.

When a young man and woman come to me seeking my advice regarding whether or not they should get married, I try to understand what brought them together in the first place. When I notice that one is attracted to the other mainly for his or her spiritual fervor, I know that this relationship will not last very long. When I share my long-standing experience with them, quite often they don't understand. Invariably, such people suffer while they are in the relationship as well as after they are separated. To live a happy life, all you have to do is identify the human within you and adore it. To have a healthy, happy relationship, discover a person in whom the human is fully awakened. A relationship between two fully grown and awakened humans will always be successful. It will be a source of happiness. Two such human beings become instrumental in bringing forth a soul with a fully awakened human in it. They are the creators of true human families and societies.

To have a happy family life, you have to cultivate trust in each other. Love receives its nourishment from trust. But do not expect everlasting stability in any worldly relationship, for everything in this world is constantly changing. The law of change applies to everything, including the mindset of the person whom you love and trust so much. Do not be disappointed when your trust in someone or something fails you. You must learn to maintain your inner repose and happiness, even at the cost of losing someone whom you trusted very much. To clarify my point, let me share one of my experiences with you.

Long before I came to the United States, I lived in Germany. There in Hamburg, I met a lovely couple. Never before had I met such handsome people. They were so beautiful that once you saw them, you could not take your eyes off them. They loved each other very much. The wife was a nurse in the same hospital where her husband worked as a doctor. Eventually, they had a child and she went on maternity leave. While she stayed at home, she learned that her husband was flirting with women. When she confronted her husband, he laughed and said assuringly, "Who in the world could be more beautiful than you? Why should I flirt with anyone?" Only half-convinced, she let it go momentarily. One day, while nursing her baby, the wife received a telephone call from her best friend at the hospital, who said, "While you are staying at home do you know what your husband is doing here?" Holding her baby to her bosom, the wife asked, "No, tell me, what is he doing?" The nurse whispered, "He is flirting with one of the nurses." First, she was shocked. Then an unbearable fury descended on her. The baby continued suckling for a few more minutes and then began crying at the top of his lungs. Still mad, the wife did not know what had upset the baby. Suddenly, she noticed the baby's eyes rolling and his lips turning blue. Before she could rush the baby to the hospital, he was dead. The autopsy revealed that the baby died from a poison similar to snake venom.

The couple loved each other very much. But their love was not supported by complete trust. It takes time for trust to take root. Until then, you have to refine your understanding of each other. During adverse conditions, you have to control your emotions. You have to be positive. You must cultivate patience so that during unexpected inner turmoil, you maintain your equilibrium. You can do that when you know how to balance your trust and mistrust. This will allow you to enhance your trust in your loved ones and not be overtly affected when your trust is shaken.

Life is full of surprises. You must be ready to react to those surprises wisely. Wisdom lies in maintaining a state of equanimity. When you expect too much from others, you lose your equilibrium. When you doubt too much, you lose your equilibrium. Both a skeptic and an overly trusting person remain frantic and miserable. People from both categories jump to conclusions too fast and later regret it. Do not run after the charms and temptations of the world, but at the same time, do not condemn them. Enjoy the objects of the world and when you are done, wash your hands of them. It is not your spouse, your children, or your career, nor the loss and gain, or the success and failure in relation to them that make you happy or miserable. Rather, it is the value that you superimpose on them that creates a world of difference.

A person lacking introspection goes on identifying himself with his successes and failures. Such a person one day becomes so empty that his world of comprehension shrinks to his worldly successes and failures. He is always frightened by the idea of losing what he had and the idea of not being able to achieve what seems to secure his existence. In this circumscribed world of fear, he goes on living. He may have all the objects of the world at his disposal, and yet the level of his insecurity and the misery caused by it makes him the poorest of the poor.

Fear caused by insecurity drains vitality from your body. It makes your mind listless. It takes away the sharpness of your intellect. Richness of thought is gone. You become weak and frail. You no longer perceive this world as beautiful. Living in this world, therefore, becomes burdensome and yet, driven by destiny, you go on living. How pitiful is this kind of life.

Sometimes people ask me, "Swamiji, how can you be free of fear when the real cause of fear is right before your eyes? How can you not suffer from anxiety when the stock market rules the economic world? How can you not be anxious when your country is at war? How can you be at peace when violence has become so pervasive? Can you be fearless when you are chased by a tiger?" The truth is that fear invites danger.

Once upon a time, I visited a sage in one of the shrines in the Himalayas called Chandra Badani. Even today, wild animals live around this shrine. I spent the whole afternoon with this saint. Then, at around four in the afternoon, the saint said, "I have to cook some food. My friends will be arriving soon." He made dough; I helped him make the fire. Then he prepared bread on the skillet, big enough for fifteen to twenty people to eat. There was still daylight, and his friends began to arrive. Do you know who they were? Jackals, foxes, and tigers. He distributed pieces of bread to these friends. We, too, had our share. Then he told them, "Today, I have a special visitor, so please, all of you, go." Thus the wild animals were gone.

In the Himalayas, villages are situated amidst wildlife, but I have never once heard of a villager being attacked by wild animals. Cattle graze in the jungle safely. Late in the night, wild animals come very close to the villages, and before dawn, they go back to their hidings places. My master told me that I should settle down before the second quarter of the night because by the time the third quarter begins, the animals become active. By the end of the third quarter, they try to come closer to human settlements. When I asked my master why they do this, he said, "Because they want to experience God's love, which has been deposited so immensely in human hearts. It is their longing for human love that brings them to the villages." It was an eye-opening message. I paid attention to what he said. Sometimes in the middle of the night, and in the early mornings, I would wake up just to see whether there were wild animals around my hut. Curled inside my blanket, I could see their shining eyes outside my hut. I was told by my master that if I saw the animals, I must not disturb them. I must not panic. I should not be scared of them, and I should not scare them. I should just be quiet and enjoy their presence just as they were enjoying mine.

Wild animals go out of their way to attack humans under only two circumstances: first, when they are threatened, and second, when a natural catastrophe is under way. Under these two circumstances, their instinct is triggered, and that is when, in a panic, they attack. Unlike animals, humans use their judgment. Their response to fear is largely based on their free will. If they decide to, they can remain calm and tranquil in the face of fearful situations, and by doing so, they can change its outcome. The reverse is true, too. They can go on brooding on a fearful idea; they can breathe life into that idea through their negativity, and soon, it turns into a living reality.

In my childhood, I was afraid of snakes. Wherever I went, I always checked whether or not there was a snake around. I used to shake my clothes before putting them on. The idea of a snake would enter my mind before I slipped my feet into my shoes. For reasons unknown to me, snakes followed me wherever I went. I was terrified. My phobia of snakes reached its climax during my teenage years. But I was embarrassed to tell anyone. One day I realized that I had better face and resolve this problem. But how? I told my master. He said, "Yes, I know what your problem is."

"Then why didn't you help me?" I asked.

"Someone can help you only after you acknowledge that you have a problem and you need help. Tomorrow, I will take care of this problem, and thereafter, you will never be afraid of snakes. Today, before sunset, gather some wildflowers. Early in the morning, I will perform a special ritual to propitiate the Lord of snakes. Thereafter, your fear of snakes will vanish forever."

Following his instructions, I gathered flowers and put them in a basket. Early in the morning, right at the outset of the rituals, my master asked me to hold the flowers in my palms. I put my hand in the basket, and in a panic, I shouted, "Snake!" In the dim light of the ceremonial lamp, I saw a snake sitting on the heap of flowers with its hood spread. My master commanded, "Pick him up! Do as I tell you. You are not his food. You have no reason to fear him."

I had no choice. I also knew that if anything happened to me, my master would have the cure. I picked up the coiled snake with its widespread hood. It kept glaring at me. My hands were shaking, and still my master ordered me to kiss the snake. I hesitated. Then he took the snake from my hands and brought the creature close to his heart. He hugged the snake as though it were a little baby, and said, "See how clean is this snake? How shiny are his eyes? How beautiful he is? All creatures, including this snake, are children of God. This snake, too, has a right to receive the same love as you do."

By this time, my fear was gone. I lovingly touched the body and then the head of the snake. Then my master placed the snake on the ground and it slithered away. This incident made me realize that it is our fear that invites danger.

Today, I see that fear has pervaded every nook and cranny of our lives. Fear has become a hallmark of our society. Instead of discovering the cause of fear, people exhaust their energy by destroying those whom they fear. Sensing our intention, the person on whom we focus our fear attacks us. Soon, both parties turn into each other's enemies. Both parties are then on the offensive, although to justify their behavior, they claim that they are acting only in self-defense. This is the simple anatomy of a dispute both at home and war in the world. If you ever wish to attain peace and happiness, you must discover the cause of your fear. This discovery will help you eliminate the very element of animosity, and your enemies will vanish once and for all. I had been holding snakes responsible for my fear. Somewhere at a very deep level, I had been telling myself that if snakes did not exist, I would be a fearless, happy person. Once I realized how faulty my understanding was, my phobia vanished and snakes stopped chasing me.

To attain freedom from fear, you don't have to kiss a cobra or feed bread to tigers. All I advise is that you look into the cause of your fear. See what is there that compels you to see others as your enemy; what is there that forces you to challenge the purity of your love for others; and what is there that holds you back and does not allow you to open yourself to others. A deep, prolonged introspection will tell you that you are afraid of losing the self-image that you hold so dear. The possibility of losing that self-image frightens you. You are always afraid that someone might alter your image, and that will be the end of your world. Paranoia caused by the prospect of losing your image forces you to be on alert all the time. Your defense mechanism is always on. This is a very painful way of living life.

The antidote to fear is love. Love means giving self-lessly. Look at the lives of all great people—all of them were fearless, for they had love for all. They shared their love selflessly and did not desire even a word of thanks from those they served. This selfless, uncondi-tional love did not spare room for any animosity in their minds and hearts. Jesus Christ was misunderstood by so many people, but it did not stop him from distributing his love. When he was being crucified, he said, "Father, forgive them, for they know not what they do." So is the case with all other great souls, be they Buddha, Krishna, or Mahatma Gandhi. Self-lessness was their strength, for they were not afraid of losing anything. They were free from the impulse of defending themselves, for they knew that the immortal within them could not be killed by anyone. It is from the depth of their self-understanding that they were able to disperse an aura of peace and tranquility. You, too, can do it. Just try, and see what happens.

In order to practice love and find peace and happi-ness, you do not need to become an activist; you do not need to demonstrate; you do not need to join an army of peacekeepers; you do not need to seek an opportunity to be crucified. Be wherever you are and do whatever you are supposed to do. However, it is up to you to decide what you are supposed to do. On the path of happiness, first pay attention to those who are near and dear to you. In your thoughts, speech, and actions, do not harm anyone, beginning with those who are closest to you. Who is closest to you? No one is closer to you than yourself. First, stop hurting yourself. You have become a champion of hurting yourself. Someone tells you that you are a bad person and without giving a second thought, you believe it. By doing so, let me tell you, you are dishonoring the greatest gift that Divine Providence has given you. That greatest gift is your conscience, the voice of your heart.

Unless you learn to hear and heed the voice of your heart, you cannot be happy. Unless you hear and heed the voice of your heart, all great Bibles of the world will remain useless to you, for you will not understand their contents and intents. You have put your conscience, the precious gift of Providence, to sleep. And yet, you assume that your teachers, preachers, and your temples and clergy will wake you up. The caretakers of these holy scriptures have been telling you that there is hell and there is heaven. If you do wrong, you go to hell. If you do right, you go to heaven. Both right and wrong are decided by those outside you. You go on living and acting in response to your urges, habits, needs, and desires. In the process, many of your actions do not seem to fit in the definition of "right." Upon realizing that you are a wrongdoer, you feel terrible. You feel guilty; you condemn yourself. You go on identifying yourself as a wrongdoer. Then you no longer have the time to examine whether or not you are really a wicked person, and you allow the whole cosmos to punish you. How much punishment can your tiny mind and heart take?

I assure you, God is not a jailer. It is your own conviction that creates a jailer for you, and it is your sheer ignorance that you call that jailer God. At the eve of my life, I say loud and clear, "A God whose functions are limited to punishing 'bad people' and to rewarding 'good people' is your creation. No one other than you can free yourself from your self-created God, hell, heaven, punishments, and rewards. Wake up! Live a responsible and purposeful life. Throw away the crutches that perpetuate your dependency on others and create a world of your choice—a world that is happy and peaceful."

God bless you.

About Swami Rama

ONE OF THE GREATEST ADEPTS, TEACHERS, writers, and humanitarians of the 20th century, Swami Rama is the founder of the Himalayan Institute. Born in Northern India, he was raised from early childhood by a Himalayan sage, Bengali Baba. Under the guidance of his master he traveled from monastery to monastery and studied with a variety of Himalayan saints and sages, including his grandmaster who was living in a remote region of Tibet. In addition to this intense spiritual training, Swami Rama received higher education in both India and Europe. From 1949 to 1952, he held the prestigious position of Shankaracharya of Karvirpitham in South India. Thereafter, he returned to his master to receive further training at his cave monastery, and finally in 1969, came to the United States where he founded the Himalayan Institute. His best known work, *Living with the Himalayan Masters*, reveals the many facets of this singular adept and demonstrates his embodiment of the living tradition of the East.

About Pandit Rajmani Tigunait, Ph.D.

PANDIT RAJMANI TIGUNAIT, PH.D., THE SPIRITUAL head of the Himalayan Institute®, is the successor of Swami Rama of the Himalayas. Lecturing and teaching worldwide for more than a quarter of a century, he is a regular contributor to *Yoga International* magazine and the author of twelve books, including the best-selling *At the Eleventh Hour: The Biography of Swami Rama of the Himalayas*.

Pandit Tigunait holds two doctorates: one in Sanskrit from the University of Allahabad in India and another in Oriental Studies from the University of Pennsylvania. Family tradition gave Pandit Tigunait access to a vast range of spiritual wisdom preserved in both the written and oral traditions. Before meeting his master, Pandit Tigunait studied Sanskrit, the language of the ancient scriptures of India, as well as the languages of the Buddhist, Jain, and Zoroastrian traditions. In 1976, Swami Rama ordained Pandit Tigunait into the 5,000-year-old lineage of the Himalayan masters.

The Himalayan Institute

The main building of the Institute headquarters near Honesdale, Pennsylvania.

FOUNDED IN 1971 BY SWAMI RAMA, the Himalayan Institute has been dedicated to helping people grow physically, mentally, and spiritually by combining the best knowledge of both the East and the West.

Our international headquarters is located on a beautiful 400-acre campus in the rolling hills of the Pocono Mountains of northeastern Pennsylvania. The atmosphere here is one to foster growth, increased inner awareness, and calm. Our grounds provide a wonderfully peaceful and healthy setting for our seminars and extended programs. Students from all over the world join us here to attend programs in such diverse areas as hatha yoga, meditation, stress reduction, Ayurveda, nutrition, Eastern philosophy, psychology, and other subjects. Whether the programs are for weekend meditation retreats, week-long seminars on spirituality, months-long residential programs, or holistic health services, the attempt here is to provide an environment of gentle inner progress.

We invite you to join with us in the ongoing process of personal growth and development.

The Institute is a nonprofit organization. Your membership in the Institute helps to support its programs. Please call or write for information on becoming a member.

PROGRAMS AND SERVICES INCLUDE:
- Weekend or extended seminars and workshops
- Meditation retreats and advanced meditation instruction
- Hatha yoga teachers' training
- Residential programs for self-development
- Holistic health services and pancha karma at the Institute's Center for Health and Healing
- Spiritual excursions
- Varcho Veda® herbal products
- Himalayan Institute Press
- *Yoga International* magazine
- Sanskrit correspondence course

A Quarterly Guide to Programs and Other Offerings is free within the USA. To request a copy, or for further information, call 800-822-4547 or 570-253-5551, write to the Himalayan Institute, 952 Bethany Turnpike, Building 1, Honesdale, PA 18431, USA, or visit our website at www.HimalayanInstitute.org

HIMALAYAN INSTITUTE® PRESS

HIMALAYAN INSTITUTE PRESS has long been regarded as "The Resource for Holistic Living." We publish dozens of titles, as well as audio and video tapes that offer practical methods for living harmoniously and achieving inner balance. Our approach addresses the whole person—body, mind, and spirit—integrating the latest scientific knowledge with ancient healing and self-development techniques.

As such, we offer a wide array of titles on physical and psychological health and well-being, spiritual growth through meditation and other yogic practices, as well as translations of yogic scriptures.

Our yoga accessories include the Japa Kit for meditation practice and the Neti Pot™, the ideal tool for sinus and allergy sufferers. Our Varcho Veda® line of quality herbal extracts is now available to enhance balanced health and well-being.

Subscriptions are available to a bimonthly magazine, *Yoga International*, which offers thought-provoking articles on all aspects of meditation and yoga, including yoga's sister science, Ayurveda.

To receive a free catalog, call 800-822-4547 or 570-253-5551, email hibooks@HimalayanInstitute.org, fax 570-647-1552, write to Himalayan Institute Press, 630 Main St., Suite 350, Honesdale, PA 18431-1843, USA, or visit our website at www.HimalayanInstitute.org.